Epistemology, Ethics, and Meaning in Unusually Personal Scholarship

Amber Esping

Epistemology, Ethics, and Meaning in Unusually Personal Scholarship

palgrave
macmillan

Amber Esping
Texas Christian University
Fort Worth, TX, USA

ISBN 978-3-030-08842-2 ISBN 978-3-319-73718-8 (eBook)
https://doi.org/10.1007/978-3-319-73718-8

Softcover re-print of the Hardcover 1st edition 2018

Printed on acid-free paper

This Palgrave Macmillan imprint is published by Springer Nature
The registered company is Springer International Publishing AG
The registered company address is: Gewerbestrasse 11, 6330 Cham, Switzerland

"This is an inspirational and informative book, illustrating how Viktor Frankl's logotherapy on search for meaning can transform several researchers' lives and significantly impact their scholarship. These stories were told in a graceful and engaging way. More importantly, Dr. Esping captures the essence of logotherapy and shows how its principles can be fruitfully applied to graduate students and professors who are turning painful personal experiences into impactful research. I highly recommend this book."

—Paul T. P. Wong, President, International Network on Personal Meaning, and Editor of *The Human Quest for Meaning: Theories, Research, and Applications*, *Existential and Spiritual Issues in Death Attitudes* (with Adrian Tomer and Grafton T. Eliason), and *Positive Psychology of Meaning and Spirituality* (with Lilian C. J. Wong, Marvin J. McDonald, and Derrick W. Klaassen)

"This is a timely yet timeless, honest and important book—perhaps one of the most noteworthy new titles on meaning, suffering and coping we've seen published for a long time. This is a treasure to be kept and shared, and to be read over and over again."

—Alexander Batthyány, Endowed Viktor Frankl Chair of Philosophy and Psychology in Liechtenstein, Director of the Viktor Frankl Institute, Vienna. Editor of the *Collected Works of Viktor Frankl*, *Existential Psychotherapy of Meaning: Handbook of Logotherapy and Existential Analysis* (with Jay Levinson), *Meaning in Positive and Existential Psychology* (with Pninit Russo-Netzer), and Author (with David Guttmann) of *Empirical Research on Logotherapy and Meaning-Oriented Psychotherapy*, and *Overcoming Indifference* (forthcoming)

"There's an expression that all research is me-search. However, for some researchers, their work is unusually personal. This book does a wonderful job, through deeply moving vignettes and discussion of Viktor Frankl's seminal work, of showing that the academy doesn't have to be dry and divorced from all meaning. In fact, Esping shows how all academics can harness their own unusually personal scholarship in ways that motivate them to do their best work."

—Scott Barry Kaufman, Author of *Ungifted: The Truth about Talent, Practice, Creativity, and the Many Paths to Greatness*

"What better way to deal with profound trial in life than to use it as a basis to derive meaning and service that will endure for a lifetime? There are few other works in my experience that address the power of such transformations within the academic world—and that could inspire many with similar challenges, to follow the Franklian example."

—Kirk Schneider, Author of *The Spirituality of Awe: Challenges to the Robotic Revolution*, *The Polarized Mind: Why It's Killing Us and What We Can Do About It*, and *Existential-Humanistic Therapy* (with Orah Krug)

"A deeply insightful and practical book about exploring one's personal life in academic research. A must read for graduate students and faculty seeking to find meaning in and convey understanding of profoundly personal situations they have experienced. Calling on Viktor Frankl's Existential Psychology, the author offers advice to scholars attracted to this approach and addresses the existential questions it raises. An excellent book for all courses dealing with personal narrative, autoethnography, and ethics."

—Carolyn Ellis, Author of *The Ethnographic I: A Methodological Novel about Autoethnography*, and *Evocative Autoethnography: Writing Lives and Telling Stories* (with Arthur Bochner)

For Sherrie Reynolds

Preface

Prominent autoethnographer Arthur Bochner believes, "There's nothing more theoretical than a good story" (Ellis 2004, p. 23). In that spirit, the present book begins with four case studies of university professors who have, or at one time had, unusually personal motivations for their research agendas. Their stories were chosen because (1) they epitomize the Existentialist ideal of the search for meaning in scholarship, and (2) their academic careers invite questions about research ethics and epistemology in situations where the researcher is viscerally connected to his or her area of scholarly expertise. These initial chapters can work as compelling, stand-alone portraits of scholarship undertaken in the interstices of the personal and the professional, the subjective and the objective, the researcher and the subject of research. The stories also serve as an empirical base for the explicitly theoretical chapters in Part II of this book.

The first two case studies are founded on longitudinal interview data and artifacts spanning more than a decade, providing a developmental perspective on young researchers' career trajectories from graduate school through tenure and promotion. The other two cases feature prominent scholars at or nearing retirement. These last two chapters in Part I provide a retrospective look at academic lives fully and meaningfully lived. I should mention at the outset that these four individuals would be worth listening to even without the special circumstances that lead to their inclusion in this book. Two have earned tenure at R1 universities. Another attained tenure at a large state school and has since been hired at an R1 university. A fourth works in a non-tenurable research position in the Ivy League. Two of the four have achieved the terminal rank of Full Professor. The others are Associate. All four have received prestigious awards for their scholarship and/or teaching. These are successful faculty members who, I hope, will serve as virtual mentors through their stories. They have abundant wisdom and advice to share with readers who have unusually personal motivations for their scholarship, as well as the rest of us who are just trying to do honorable, meaningful, and impactful work in the academy. To this end, each Case Study is followed by a bulleted list of advice for graduate students, faculty advisors, or both.

Part II of this book deals with questions of epistemology and ethics in unusually personal research. Using the case studies in Part I as a foundation, we will interrogate concepts relating to technical aspects of Franklian thought. Chapter 6 begins with an introduction to Viktor Frankl's existential psychology, also known as logotherapy. This framework offers it its own epistemology, and this is the subject of Chapter 7. Chapter 8, "Ethical Dilemmas in Unusually Personal Research" explores some perceived advantages and disadvantages for researchers who have unusually personal connections to their subjects of inquiry.

In the academy, we do not create résumés. We build *vitas.* Perhaps some of us are using this word too narrowly. The final two chapters are founded on the idea that in Latin, the word *vita* means "life." Viktor Frankl's existential psychology is, at its core, a theory of motivation. Understanding the ways in which the search for meaning motivates us can be genuinely helpful in creating a fulfilling and prolific academic *vita.* Certainly, one focus of this book is to ask the questions: Reader, what meaning does your scholarship bring to your life? And more importantly, what meaning does your life bring to your scholarship? Chapter 9 lays out Frankl's motivational theory. Chapter 10, "The Search for Meaning in the Academy" helps put this into context. Each chapter in Part II ends with a section called "Existential Questions for Readers," which is an invitation to consider the personal relevance of major themes from the chapter.

This book is written with several readerships in mind. First, it should be useful for researchers with unusually personal connections to their scholarship. It is my aim to support you in your academic career by providing ethical and epistemological support that can be used to justify, promote, and improve your work. I believe you can be a serious scholar or scientist and still have a warm, beating heart. But I also believe you can make mistakes that can hurt you and your field if you don't really know what you are doing, or you don't do it boldly. I am also hoping to engage the more traditionally motivated scholars working alongside you, evaluating your scholarship, hiring you, or deciding whether to grant you tenure. Their concerns about the rigor of your scholarship are legitimate and deserve thoughtful, well-reasoned responses. We should not try to convince them that your background or motivation should not be pause for concern, but I do believe that we can show ways in which your background and motivation can be exceptionally helpful for advancing the field if it handled appropriately.

I am also writing to the skeptics, to those of you who are uber-positivist scholars, who see no place at all for emotion or personal lived experience in scholarship. This book is not likely to change your epistemological or ethical stance, and I'm not sure I want it to. But I would like to engage you in a conversation. Because as it turns out, it *is* possible to espouse positivism or near-positivism and still have very personal—even heart-wrenching—reasons for conducting research on a particular topic. And there may be ways to use those reasons to advance the work. Here is the bottom line: If a story about a tenured theoretical physicist who wants to build a time machine to save his dad from a fatal heart attack sounds a little crazy to you, (Chapter 4) then it is probably best to disregard the backstory and evaluate the work of said scientist based on other (positivist) criteria and see where it lands. You might just be surprised by how very good it is.

Fort Worth, TX, USA — Amber Esping

Reference

Ellis, C. (2004). *The ethnographic I: A methodological novel about autoethnography.* Walnut Creek, CA: AltaMira.

Acknowledgements

Gratitude is considered by many Franklian-oriented existential psychologists to be an experiential value through which we can discover meaning in our lives. I agree. There are abundant reasons to be thankful for this project, for the existential purposes it has served in my professional journey, and for the many generous souls who have contributed meaningfully to its realization. First and foremost, this work is dedicated to Dr. Sherrie Reynolds (1942–2014), who was a superb model for creating and maintaining an intellectually nourishing, prolific, and warmly generative academic career. When I was a junior faculty member unreasonably fixated on tenure requirements, she provided a centering influence. She showed by example that it is possible to privilege kindness in the academy. Thank you, Sherrie, from the bottom of my heart.

Dr. Mary Patton, Dean of the College of Education at Texas Christian University, and Dr. Nowell Donovan, TCU Provost, offered the gift of time to begin this work by providing sabbatical leave in the fall of 2016. The TCU College of Education and Ms. Maryett Vansau Thompson (TCU Class of 1970) supported its development through a 2015 Summer Research Program Grant, as did TCU Office of Sponsored Programs' Junior Faculty Summer Research Program and Research and Creative Activities Fund Grants in 2009. This early backing jumpstarted some of the foundational research for this book.

I am also truly appreciative of my TCU colleagues, most especially for the time spent sharing ideas, goals, and laughter while writing together at our homes and on retreat. As I type these acknowledgments, computers, books, glasses, and about a dozen faculty members are splayed across various couches and tables in a lovely woodland cabin. Winding up this paragraph, I look forward to more laughter, inspiration, and plentiful wine with our dinner. Y'all are an important reason why TCU is one of the Great Colleges to Work For. (And a huge thank you to Mark and Jo Beth Southard for welcoming us into your gorgeous lake house!)

The origins of this book began with my dissertation. I will forever be grateful to several faculty members at Indiana University, Bloomington, for their profound and enduring influence. In particular, Dr. Jonathan Plucker (now at Johns Hopkins) was a generous, insightful, and encouraging mentor who continues to inspire students and colleagues through his example of a brilliant and prolific researcher who is also just a really wonderful—and very funny—human being. Dr. Phil Carspecken, Dr. Barbara Dennis, and Dr. David Flinders shaped my thinking about qualitative epistemology, methodology, and ethics, and it is always my aim to treat my students like these mentors treated me. I always smile when I hear their words coming out of my mouth. Dr. Ann V. Graber directed my study at the Viktor Frankl Institute of Logotherapy, and her enthusiasm for diverse cultural and religious perspectives on personal meaning remains foundational in my thinking about Franklian existential psychology practice in the twenty-first century. From Ann, I also learned a great deal about living a rich and meaningful life personally.

I am also immensely grateful for Rachel Krause, commissioning editor at Palgrave Macmillan, who invited me to write this book, and to my very helpful editorial assistant, Kyra Saniewski, for making the publication process seamless and stress-free.

Heartfelt thanks to Lilli Erickson. You have helped me to enjoy the "prestige of the center," so I hope you are now enjoying the prestige of the front of a book. You are a gifted teacher and coach, and your presence in my life made this project a lot easier to accomplish. I knew that after long hours at the computer I had something completely different and wonderful look forward to. I'm eager to see more of you now that it is finished! Thank you.

Bountiful thanks are due to my family—Thomas, Dylan, Lara, Gilbert, Mary, Michael E, Nancy, Merideth, Michael S—and the folks at Euless First United Methodist Church. You are my *logos*. I love you to Texas and back. Special thanks to Thomas, who is a talented writer with a sensitive ear for beautiful language and clarity of expression. He read every word of the manuscript, red pen in hand. Thomas, this book, like my life, is exponentially better because I am married to you.

Finally, my deepest appreciation to the interview participants, both named and unnamed, who appear in this book. Thank you for allowing me to be a steward of your stories. I hope I have honored this gift as you have honored me by giving of your time and your humanity.

Fort Worth, TX, USA Amber Esping
October 2017

Contents

List of Figures

PART I

Case Studies

CHAPTER 1

Introduction to Part I: Warming the Room, Turning on the Lights

The impetus for this book comes from a story told by the psychiatrist, neurologist, and existential philosopher Viktor Emil Frankl (1905–1997) in his riveting Holocaust narrative, *Man's Search for Meaning*.[1] A prisoner for three years in the Theresienstadt, Auschwitz, and two Dachau-affiliated concentration camps, he wrote about his own suffering from two, typically incommensurable, perspectives—the scientist and the subject of study. In the following passage, he describes the genesis of this work:

> Almost in tears from pain (I had terrible sores on my feet from wearing torn shoes), I limped a few kilometers with our long column of men from the camp to our work site. Very cold, bitter winds struck us. I kept thinking of the endless little problems of our miserable life. What would there be to eat tonight? If a piece of sausage came as extra ration, should I exchange it for a piece of bread? ….How could I get a piece of wire to replace the fragment which served as one of my shoelaces? Would I get to our work site in time to join my usual working party or would I have to join another, which might have a brutal foreman?…
> I became disgusted with the state of affairs which compelled me, daily and hourly, to think of only such trivial things. I forced my thoughts to turn to another subject. Suddenly I saw myself standing on the platform of a well-lit, warm and pleasant lecture room. In front of me sat an attentive

[1] Frankl's books were written and translated during a historical period when it was acceptable to use the word "man" inclusively to mean "human beings." I will retain "man" in order to preserve the integrity of Frankl's quotes. Elsewhere I will use "human beings."

A. Esping, *Epistemology, Ethics, and Meaning in Unusually Personal Scholarship*, https://doi.org/10.1007/978-3-319-73718-8_1

> audience on comfortable upholstered seats. I was giving a lecture on the psychology of the concentration camp! All that oppressed me at that moment became objective, seen and described from the remote viewpoint of science. By this method I succeeded somehow in rising ... above the sufferings of the moment, and I observed them as if they were already of the past. Both I and my troubles became the object of an interesting psychoscientific study undertaken by myself. What does Spinoza say in his Ethics?... "Emotion, which is suffering, ceases to be suffering as soon as we form a clear and precise picture of it". (Frankl 1946/2014, pp. 68–69)

When he entered the camps, Frankl was already an expert on human suffering. By dint of years of education and practice, most psychiatrists are. A precocious scholar, he began a regular correspondence with Sigmund Freud while he was still in high school. His first academic journal article was published shortly thereafter. He developed his own existential approach to psychotherapy, which by 1926 had come to be called "logotherapy." When he arrived in Auschwitz in 1944, he was carrying the only manuscript for a book on this topic sewn into the lining of his overcoat. Frankl was forced to abandon the coat and its secret cargo as he entered the camp (Frankl 1995/2000).

Devastated by the loss of his *magnum opus*, he set a goal of reconstructing the manuscript. He began by scribbling notes on some pilfered SS forms. Sick with typhus and near death, he believed that the meaning he discovered in this undertaking helped to keep him from succumbing to despair. He finished reconstructing the book after liberation, and in English, it is called *The Doctor and the Soul* (1955/1986). It is, however, a different book than the original. In light of his recent experiences, it had to be.

Frankl's imprisonment gave him an insider's perspective on suffering that his pre-war academic and clinical training could never have manifested. Psychiatrists writing from the outside might meaningfully capture the substance of the concentration camp experience, but they could never truly enter its depths. Former prisoners who were not also psychiatrists would know the depths, but they could not interpret and communicate their experiences in the language and conventions of the field. As an insider with academic training, Frankl could do both. And for the next half-century he did. He came closer than I have ever seen anyone in describing the ineffable for other experts who haven't "been there." His research, writing, and teaching revealed a courageous intersectionality of his dual identities of "objective" scientist and "subjective" sufferer. He truly gave his scholarship all of himself, and it saved his life (Frankl 1995/2000).

In this respect, Frankl is not alone. There are faculty members writing and teaching in well-lit, warm rooms in universities across the globe who are manifesting Frankl's vision. They are using the tools of rigorous scholarly inquiry to form "clear and precise pictures" of issues intimately related to their own experiences of suffering or loss, or to confront big existential questions surrounding other complicated personal experiences. Done well, their publications offer exceptionally nuanced, multidimensional perspectives that educate other scholars who haven't "been there." They are models of scholarly erudition that pay careful attention to issues of epistemology and ethics. Done poorly, their publications may serve as warnings that push other scholars with unusually personal motivations for their scholarly agendas underground.

Part I of this book will introduce several individuals who have unusually personal connections to their areas of study. In Chapter 2, we will meet Gillian, a young bereaved mother who studied other bereaved parents for her doctoral dissertation research. Now an associate research scientist at an Ivy League university, she no longer studies bereavement. But the opportunity to do so for four years during graduate school honed her research skills (to the degree that she landed an Ivy League job!), and yielded generalizable insights that have been used to help others who work with bereaved parents. Just as important, reading and interpreting various perspectives on grief played an integral part in moving her forward in her own grief process. For Gillian, graduate school was profoundly therapeutic, but also an experience she was eager to leave behind after graduation.

In Chapter 3, we will meet Jesse, a transgender social scientist whose Ph.D. dissertation involved studying issues related to "atypically-gendered" people—his preferred term for individuals like himself. In addition to teaching statistics at an R1[2] university, he is now an award-winning LGBT+ advocate who travels the country speaking about sex and gender. While aspects of graduate school were painful for Jesse (such as having to scrap his original dissertation topic very late in the game because his Chair would not support some of his premises), his academic work contributed meaningfully to his self-understanding. Moreover, his many opportunities to give class presentations and speak on campus facilitated his coming-out process.

[2] R1 is the Carnegie classification for universities with the highest research productivity.

But what of researchers in the "hard" sciences? They also may have unusually personal motivations for their research agendas. In Chapter 4, we will meet Ronald L. Mallett, a theoretical physicist who became fascinated by time travel at age 11 when he encountered a 1956 comic book rendering of H. G. Wells' novel, *The Time Machine* (Wells 1895/2017). Ron's father had died unexpectedly a year earlier, and the concept of time travel seemed to offer a way back to him. Ron used radio tubes, television parts, and pieces of bicycles to build a time machine in his basement. Of course this first attempt did not work—but building a time machine remained his unwavering goal when he began a Ph.D. program and joined the ranks of academe. Now a well-known expert on black holes and cosmology and an emeritus full professor of theoretical physics, he realizes that his goal will not be realized in his lifetime. But he still believes it will happen. His technical papers never mention the origin story of this work, but the complex equations filling the pages are implicit testimony to a lonely little boy's 60-year quest to see his father again.

Sometimes the relationships between the personal and the scholarly evolve across the breadth of a distinguished academic career. In the final chapter of Part I, we will hear from Margaret Pabst "Peggy" Battin, a renowned bioethicist and champion of self-determination in dying. One question drives her scholarship: "Why should it be so hard to die?" It was Peggy's mother who posed this question. Peggy was a junior in college, and her mother was at the tail end of a lingering and painful death from cancer. A key player in right-to-die legislation, Peggy has since helped make death easier for some people. However, the issue became acutely personal yet again when, about 50 years after she first pondered that formative question, Peggy's husband was horrifically injured in a bicycle accident. She paraphrased Dostoevsky's Ivan Ilych in a subsequent autoethnographic publication, "What if my whole life has been wrong?" Her straightforward answer is no. But bioethics issues related to autonomy in dying became far more nuanced and complicated when viewed from her husband's bedside.

In two of the four cases, I have used the participants' real names. The two senior scholars, Ron Mallett and Peggy Battin have achieved a level of prominence in their fields that makes it difficult to dis-identify them. The younger scholars, Jesse and Gillian, preferred that I create pseudonyms and obscure some minor details, and I have done this. These faculty members represent a range of disciplines: health behavior (Gillian), social sciences[3] (Jesse), theoretical physics (Ron), and bioethics (Peggy). Two of the participants are female. One is male. One is a transgender male. Geographically, they live in the West, the Midwest, and New England. Three of the four stories revolve around the death of loved ones—Gillian's son, Ron's father, Peggy's mother and husband. Jesse's story of scholarship with and for atypically gendered individuals provides contrast by highlighting a different impetus for an academic focus rooted in personal pain.

Reader, let me pause for a moment to address something, because I know some of you are starting to get worried. Despite the stories about loss and pain that follow, *this is not a sad book.* Take heart. Yes, there are some sad stories here. Tears were shed during some of the interviews, and it wasn't just my participants who cried. But there was also a lot of laughter. It is my aim that you finish Part I feeling inspired by the participants' dedication, and eager to discover more meaning in your own scholarship going forward—even if your research agenda is motivated purely by intellectual curiosity. In Part II, you'll learn a great deal about Frankl's existential framework for interpreting, evaluating, and executing unusually personal scholarship. This should be an intellectually and emotionally challenging experience, but not a distressing one. My goal is that you finish this book feeling a renewed sense of purpose and enthusiasm for your academic work.

Theoretical Framework Assumed in This Book

This book employs the lens of Viktor Frankl's existential psychology—called "logotherapy"—as it is presented in *Man's Search for Meaning* (Frankl 1946/2014), *The Doctor and the Soul* (Frankl 1955/1986), and *The Will To Meaning* (Frankl 1969/2014).

Part I relies on a specific image derived from Frankl's work—that of the "well-lit, warm and pleasant lecture room" as an interpretive metaphor. Part II provides a more in-depth exploration of Franklian thought as it relates to unusually personal scholarship. Briefly, logotherapy can be defined as "healing through meaning" (Frankl 1969/2014, p. xviii) or as "an existential type of psychotherapy which maintains that [a person's] mental health depends on awareness of meaning in his life" (Simpson and Weiner 1989). As for what "meaning" is, keep reading! For our purposes in the present book, I will take some liberties with Frankl's assertion and state my claim more narrowly:

[3] Jesse's specific discipline is obscured to protect his identity.

A researcher's mental health depends—in part—on an awareness of meaning in her scholarship.

Personally, I believe this is true for Gillian, Jesse, Ron, and Peggy. I also believe it to be true for the rest of us.

A Brief Note on Methodology and Voice

The empirical portions of this book were derived from a critical ethnographic analysis of semi-structured cross-sectional and longitudinal interview data and artifacts. I used methods of data analysis and interpretation developed by Carspecken (1996), which in turn are based on Jürgen Habermas' *Theory of Communicative Action* (1981). This methodology provides a meticulous set of procedures for gathering evidence to support truth claims in qualitative inquiry, and I have attempted to be conscientious in following these guidelines. Sarah Lawrence-Lightfoot's portraiture methodology (1997) was also highly influential in crafting the Case Study chapters.

Moreover, during the more than 10 years it took to complete the longitudinal case studies with Gillian and Jesse, I was able to build trust as I immersed myself in our shared culture of academia; as a fellow university professor, I have embraced the role of complete member researcher with all of the validity advantages insider status may confer (Adler and Adler 1987; see also Ellis 2004). With Ron and Peggy, I did not have the opportunity for prolonged engagement or persistent observation (Lincoln and Guba 1985). However, my visits with these professors included unstructured periods to build trust and empathy. For example, I have more than five hours of taped interview with Peggy Battin, but among my most vivid memories of that trip is our impromptu hike into the foothills of the Wasatch Mountain Range. The mountains did not inspire much talk about research, but I believe they helped us understand one another.

Finally, an essential check on the validity of any inferences, interpretations, or judgments in the representations in this book is member checking (see Carlson 2010; Carspecken 1996; Koelsch 2013). Jesse, Ron, and Peggy were co-constructors of their individual chapters, providing feedback on the interview transcripts and drafts of their case studies. They have each endorsed the final versions as they are presented here. For reasons that will become apparent in Chapter 2, Gillian declined my invitation to provide member checking.

References

Adler, P. A., & Adler, P. (1987). *Membership roles in field research*. Newbury Park, CA: Sage.

Carlson, J. A. (2010). Avoiding traps in member checking. *The Qualitative Report, 15*(5), 1102–1113.

Carspecken, P. F. (1996). *Critical ethnography in educational research: A theoretical and practical guide*. New York: Routledge.

Ellis, C. (2004). *The ethnographic I: A methodological novel about autoethnography*. Walnut Creek, CA: AltaMira.

Frankl, V. E. (1946/2014). *Man's search for meaning*. Boston: Beacon Press.

Frankl, V. E. (1955/1986). *The doctor and the soul*. New York: Vintage Books.

Frankl, V. E. (1969/2014). *The will to meaning: Foundations and applications of logotherapy*. New York: Meridian.

Frankl, V. E. (1995/2000). *Recollections: An autobiography* (J. Fabry & J. Fabry, Trans.). Cambridge: Basic Books.

Habermas, J. (1981). *Theory of communicative action, volume one: Reason and the rationalization of society*. Boston, MA: Beacon Press.

Koelsch, L. E. (2013). Reconceptualizing the member check interview. *International Journal of Qualitative Methods, 12*(1), 168–179.

Lawrence-Lightfoot, S., & Davis, J. H. (1997). *The art and science of portraiture*. San Francisco: Jossey-Bass.

Lincoln, Y. S., & Guba, E. (1985). *Naturalistic inquiry*. Thousand Oaks, CA: Sage.

Simpson, J. A., & Weiner, E. (Eds.). (1989). *The Oxford English Dictionary*. Oxford: Clarendon Press.

Wells, H. G. (1895/2017). *The time machine*. Seattle, WA: Amazon Classics.

Wells, H. G. (1956/2008). *Classics illustrated: The time machine* (#133). Toronto: Jack Lake Productions.

CHAPTER 2

Health Behavior: Honoring My Little Boy's Memory

"'Emotion, which is suffering, ceases to be suffering as soon as we form a clear and precise picture of it'… It's very true…Every day I think about Timothy and my loss. But as soon as I write it down it becomes very real, but it's out of my head. And it's on paper. And it serves a purpose of becoming something. Everything that I'm feeling and the pain and all of that, it has a purpose once it becomes something real, tangible for somebody else, whether it's my writing or whether I'm getting up and giving a lecture or I have a story or something. Timothy becomes real and…he's not forgotten."
—Gillian, Ph.D. Student/Bereavement Researcher, 2007

"'Emotion, which is suffering, ceases to be suffering as soon as we form a clear and precise picture of it'… I don't know if I agree with that. I don't know if it's that easy, that we can just remove ourselves and look at it… Maybe I just can't detach yet. Maybe one day it will feel that way…But I don't know if I agree with that. It doesn't cease to feel like suffering as soon as we're able to kind of step out of it. At least not for me, anyway. I mean I wish it was that easy! I wish it were that easy, that you could just put your brain into a different place. Because I don't think that's realistic for anybody."
—Gillian, Ivy League Educational Technology Researcher, 2017

My most recent interview with Gillian took place at a picnic table on a beautiful east coast beach. The brilliant sky and the sounds of frolicking children around us belied the reason for our conversation. I was here to ask Gillian some questions about a boundless loss, and to find the

A. Esping, *Epistemology, Ethics, and Meaning in Unusually Personal Scholarship*, https://doi.org/10.1007/978-3-319-73718-8_2

answer to a disquieting mystery. The last time I saw Gillian, she was in graduate school learning to conduct research with parents who had, like herself, lost children. Her decision was motivated at first by her personal desire to understand deeply "the emotions behind what it meant to be a bereaved parent," but she was also a passionate advocate for other mourning parents. She hadn't received the kind of help she needed in the aftermath of her six-year-old son Timothy's death, and she wanted to make big changes in the field. More than anything, she wanted to honor Timothy's life by making sure that counselors, educators, and the general public had a better understanding of this particularly devastating form of grief. Through this academic work, Gillian's life would become "a living memorial" to her son. Graduate school was her all-consuming mission.

That was 10 years ago. In the intervening decade, I had learned through informal means that Gillian was no longer studying bereavement. Immediately after earning her Ph.D., she had landed a prestigious post doc position at an Ivy League university and was eventually hired on there as the Deputy Director of a laboratory that develops and evaluates educational technology. *Educational technology?* When I initially interviewed her during her first and third years of graduate school, it seemed unfathomable that she would build an academic career studying anything other than parental bereavement. But I guessed now that researching and speaking on this topic had proven to be too much for her to bear—it certainly would have been so for me—and I was eager to hear her story. I had often thought about Gillian since our initial meetings, and I was a little worried about her.

Gillian is stunning. She has huge blue eyes, corn-silk blonde hair, and at 42 I'm sure she can still turn heads on the sidewalk. Recently remarried, she lives in a charming colonial home within a short commute to her Ivy League university. She seems much happier than when I knew her before; her voice is more modulated, and she is quicker to laugh. She occasionally drives a convertible. But within the first five minutes of our interview, I have already made her cry. I remember now how this goes. I cry a little too. She is imminently gracious about it, even though I—like a blockhead—have forgotten to pack the tissues in my research bag. I must *always* carry tissues for these interviews. Here is Gillian's story.

Graduate School

Gillian's son Timothy was born with a unique constellation of heart defects, and the physicians treating the little boy could not tell the family what to expect. Timothy experienced his first surgery when he was 12 hours old, and from that point, the family lived "month by month" and from surgery to surgery. In January of Timothy's sixth year, he had a heart attack. He recovered, but in March he died from complications of what should have been a very minor surgical procedure. Despite the uncertainty with which they had lived since Timothy's birth, Gillian described his death as "unexpected" and it is still unexplained. At the family's request, no autopsy was performed. "At that point," Gillian noted as her eyes welled up, "It didn't seem to matter…it wasn't like we needed a definite answer. I think after he'd been through so much …we just wanted him left alone."

Six months after Timothy died, Gillian applied for a graduate program in health behavior, with the objective of focusing on parental bereavement. Her decision was motivated at first by a desire to understand her new identity:

> It's defining in who you become, and who you are. It's part of who you are. And I think it's a part of who you are that remains with you forever. So you're not just bereaved in the sense of bereaved for a year, or bereaved for six months. You're bereaved for a lifetime…It becomes who you are so you need to understand what that means, essentially. So that's where [my application to graduate school] started…To understand, you know, the emotions behind what it meant to be a bereaved parent.

Self-understanding was not Gillian's only goal for graduate school. She also wanted to advocate for other bereaved parents and educate professionals and the general public about grief.

The statement of purpose she wrote for her application indicated that she sought to "advocate for families going through…grief" and that she wanted "to work alongside these families, to educate, to guide, to support" them. In the aftermath of her son's death, Gillian's grieving process was made more difficult by feelings of isolation. Her family and friends were "right there" for her during the first few weeks of her grief, but as time progressed she found herself increasingly alone. She could tell that the well-meaning people around her didn't know how to talk or react to her, and she felt pushed by others to "move on" and get back to her routine. They told her how to feel, how to act, and what to do. As time progressed, Gillian came to understand that she was not "getting over" her loss the way those around her expected her to. What she was feeling didn't jibe with what the people around her were telling her she should feel, so she decided to look elsewhere for help. She began "reading and writing" and doing her own "personal research" on the grieving process. She ultimately came to the conclusion that "what people *tell* you about bereavement is just—just wrong."

Academic Roles

Gillian believed graduate school would prepare her for two professional roles: bereavement teacher and researcher. In her role as researcher, Gillian felt it would be important to "be a part of the changing theories and views on bereavement." She was "excited" to be involved in the shift away from Freudian theories and Elizabeth Kübler-Ross's (1969) stage theory of grief,[1] both of which she adamantly rejected:

> There's just been this huge *shift* in death and loss and grief, and I'm excited to be a part of that…the whole Freudian [idea] that you have to cut all ties from the deceased before you can emotionally move on. And Elizabeth Kübler-Ross has the five stages…Most people if you ask them, that's how they associate their bereavement.

Gillian's desired role of researcher was closely intertwined with her role as teacher. After explaining that her research aimed to shift the focus from Freud and Kübler-Ross, she lamented that these theories are the only ones people know:

> That's all they know. It's because that's kind of what they've been *taught*. And I want to *change* that. I want to change that. No, you don't go through these nice stages, and it's not a "process" that you get over.

[1] Kübler-Ross's original formulation of her stage theory of grief suggested that grieving people progress through five stages: denial, anger, bargaining, depression, and acceptance. She later clarified that these stages may occur in any order.

Gillian supported her desire to educate teachers, students, counselors, and especially bereaved parents "about what grief is" by explaining that members of these groups do not have access to adequate resources:

> I just don't think we have enough grief education in the schools, hospitals, and colleges... the textbooks that you get—Even mine, when I teach my students—There's a tiny little section on death and dying. It's about a chapter long, ten pages. The only thing that they ever really talk about are Elizabeth Kübler-Ross's five stages of grieving, [and] I think that sets so many people up to *fail*, or disappoint, or frustrate or confuse people when they actually go through a loss and they're not following what they've been taught.

Gillian's justifications for researching and teaching about bereavement closely intersected with her acquired identity as a bereaved parent. Her dissatisfaction with Kübler-Ross's five-stage theory can be traced to her lived experience in the hours and days and years after her son died. This synergy between personal experience and research agenda is evident in the following quote. The reader should note that Gillian used the word "you" generically; she was speaking of other bereaved parents at the same time she was speaking about herself:

> The way that people treat bereaved parents...it's just a very isolating feeling. ...And you're expected to go back to work. And you're kind of pushed—People are pushing you to—"It's time to move on." Or "You need to do this"...and after a year or so, when you realize you're not moving on, you're not getting over your child, your life is not normal again... it doesn't make sense what society's been telling you. So you kind of have to look elsewhere. So that's kind of where I started reading and writing and kind of doing my *own*, personal research. I realized what people *tell* you is just wrong.

In her roles as researcher and teacher, Gillian clearly placed high value on the unique insight she possessed as a bereaved parent. From her coursework, she was gaining an academic understanding of the important problems in the field, but in her interviews with me and the class papers she provided as artifacts, she focused more on the wisdom and empathy gained from her unique lived experience. One way to interpret this is that when evaluating the relative worth of the aspects of her double consciousness (see Du Bois 1887, 1903/1944; see also Reed-Danahay 1997) as social scientist and sufferer, Gillian assigned greater importance to her identity as a bereaved parent.

Education as Power

Gillian believed that an advanced degree would provide power in the form of cultural capital[2] and that this power could be used in the service of her stated goals of helping other bereaved parents and educating professionals and the general public about grief. She formulated this by stating that she wanted an education in order to make sure that the voices of grieving families are "heard." This metaphor of getting a "voice heard" was repeated six times in Gillian's first interview with me, and one time in her second interview a year later, but in these cases the "voice" metaphor was used to explain that her decision to apply to graduate school was motivated by a strong desire to get her *own* voice heard. This shift to first person may indicate Gillian's close identification with the people she was trying to help and/or an implicit acknowledgment of her own sense of developing expertise. Gillian also stated twice in her first interview that she believed she needed an education to make her voice "louder." This belief is echoed in her master's degree application, where she said, "I feel with more education, more guidance from my faculty and respected others in the field I can pursue my goals of making a difference and changing the difficult paths that so many parents like myself have been forced to walk with such little guidance." In her Ph.D. application written a year later, Gillian explicitly juxtaposed the metaphor of getting her voice "heard" and her desire for more schooling: "I want my voice to be heard, but I want my voice to be strong and educated as well."

Meaningful Experiences in Graduate School

An analysis of the words Gillian used spontaneously to describe her experience when still in graduate school revealed only positive descriptors. This was true despite the many specific elements of graduate school she described as being difficult or painful. The words Gillian chose were: powerful (7 times); intense (2 times); cathartic (2 times); really neat (1 time); therapeutic (1 time); and interesting (1 time). She also stated her belief that she was "supposed to be here" five times.

Gillian also provided several concrete examples of meaningful experiences that helped explain her overall positive outlook. It is notable, however, that Gillian's depictions of meaningful experiences frequently

[2]Cultural capital is a sociological concept describing educational or intellectual attainments that promote social mobility (see Bourdieu and Passeron 1986).

contained both positive and negative elements and that both the positive and negative aspects were described in superlative language. These seeming contradictions serve to illustrate the complex and sometimes paradoxical process of using graduate study to find meaning in suffering; for example, Gillian described presenting at the Association of Death Education and Counseling (ADEC) conference as something she "loved" that was also "terrifying." In another example, she noted that the process of writing about death and grief for her courses was "therapeutic" and also "absolutely draining" emotionally.

The Bad Counseling Experience

One of the first meaningful experiences related to Gillian's work in graduate school occurred during her first semester in the master's program. During a counseling session, Gillian's therapist—who had lived through the loss of two of her own children—told Gillian should feel "lucky" that she didn't lose both of her children, and that she should feel "grateful" that she still had one child left. Gillian recalled her response in the quote below:

> I was *so* frustrated and angry at this woman for the things she was telling me, because they were—They were *wrong*. They weren't what I had learned in school. And to be able to walk out and...*know* that that was wrong. And it made me sad to think of another bereaved parent that perhaps didn't have the education to understand that that was wrong. To think that *she* would be going in there, and walking away with that information, and feeling guilty for feeling the feelings she was having that she had lost her child, when "Oh. Look at this poor woman that lost *two* children. I feel guilty now for—for missing my *one* child"...It was very powerful to walk away and know that...I had the education enough to say, "This wasn't *helpful* at all. This could have been more damaging than it was helpful."

Two significant elements are present in Gillian's response to her counselling experience. First, this quote provides evidence that even very early on in her program her academic work was having a positive impact on her personal mental health. Having studied bereavement formally in school, she had it on authority that what the counselor told her was "wrong." This minimized the psychological damage from the event. Gillian felt "frustrated and angry" about the situation, but she was also able to discover meaning in this event by acknowledging her burgeoning expertise in the field of grief. The second noteworthy element in Gillian's response is that she immediately tied her own painful experience to the plight of other bereaved parents who do not have access to the information Gillian had. This self-transcendence is what motivated Gillian to work hard to make her voice "louder," and this was also personally healing. Her alarming experience with the counselor reaffirmed the value of her academic efforts. When graduate school was difficult (which it frequently was), Gillian could look back to incidents such as this one to find the motivation to keep moving forward toward the Ph.D.

Researching and Writing for Class Assignments and Research Projects

One of the things Gillian found most meaningful in graduate school was the opportunity to research, read, and write about bereaved parents. In particular, she felt relief when encountering research findings that validated her own experience of loss. Prior to starting graduate school, she had felt pressure to "move on," "get over it," and feel "grateful" for the six years that she did have with her son. She wasn't "getting over" it, and worries about being "crazy" compounded her grief. Working on academic projects helped liberate her from the idea that she should be moving on:

> You read in the literature where research shows that parents *never* get over the loss of their child. You know, 35 *years* after the death of your child, people are still not getting over it…To be able to read that is very powerful because you're like, *wow*… [*sigh*] I don't *have to* get over my son. Because that's impossible anyway. But to actually *read* it…when you can sit and read that 70 other parents in a qualitative study, this is what they come up with. And it's exactly how you feel, or very close to how you feel. It's very validating…It releases a lot. It makes you feel *okay* to have the feelings that you feel…Because you know, a lot of times you do feel like you're crazy. Like, I'm gonna be depressed like this forever. You know, am I gonna cry forever? And it's just validating to know that that's okay. It's *okay* to feel this way.

Reading and writing about grief and loss in graduate school was not an entirely positive experience for Gillian. The empathy that she felt for the bereaved parents she encountered in publications and data sets often made her academic work painful. Sometimes working on school projects was "emotionally…absolutely draining":

> [*Sigh*] Well I mean [*sigh*]...having to sit down and write a 30 page paper on death and dying...when you're not *emotionally* in a place where you're feeling like writing it. Or you *read* things and it just—everything you read...is pertaining to you and your experience, or how you feel. Or you *understand*. You have this empathy for what other people are feeling... And it all makes sense—It just makes sense on a different level than somebody...maybe researching something from the outside. So it becomes very—It just becomes very personal. And it's just *an entire year* of intense writing and researching. It's just draining.

Researching and writing about bereavement was especially difficult for Gillian around "key holidays or anniversaries, or birthdays":

> There are certain times when it's harder...Like after I get through the anniversary of Timothy's death, maybe about by April 1st, from then until October I'm great. As soon [as] Halloween hits, then Thanksgiving, then Christmas and then New Years, Timothy's birthday—You know that part, it's like pulling teeth to just sit down and write. And I found it's really, really hard. And I've had to get extensions on things many times just because I *cannot* pick it up and look at it for the life of me...Timothy's been gone for over three years now. I still find sometimes it's just too emotional.

Gillian's data do not indicate that she experienced cognitive dissonance from the paradox that reading and writing about parental bereavement was "*so* therapeutic," "validating," and a "release" while it was also sometimes "draining," "like pulling teeth" and "very, very hard." It appears that her search for meaning was served through both the positive and negative aspects of the experience. She discovered meaning when she found validation and personal comfort in other peoples' data, and her self-transcendent goal of helping other bereaved parents was a strong motivation to persevere even when reading about these data was painful. Another vivid example of how meaning was derived from this complex juxtaposition of positive and negative follows.

Teaching and Presenting

Gillian also found meaning in public speaking. She did not indiscriminately share her experiences with classmates during informal socializing, but she acknowledged that some of them probably knew her story from "the grapevine." However, on several occasions she told the story of her loss in class presentations for her courses in human development and family studies. She found these talks profoundly meaningful because in doing them, she was honoring Timothy's memory and acting as a "living memorial" to her son. Gillian also stated that in helping her audience of graduate students to see that "*this* is what it means to be bereaved" she was attaining her goal of getting her voice "heard" and helping other bereaved parents:

> Because a lot of people don't feel comfortable [around bereaved people] and they don't know how [to treat them].... As soon as somebody finds out you've lost a child they become very scared of what they're going to say...So I was hoping my voice would be heard. That you know, it's *okay*. ...as [bereaved] parents we don't *need* you to say something...we want you to listen. We just want you to listen to our story. So *that's* been meaningful. And it's been meaningful to put into writing my own words. Because you see it, you think it, and you feel it, and then when you see it written it all comes together. Especially when you can pull other, like you know, literature and *research* into your own thought. It just comes together very powerfully.

Gillian also addressed the topics of grief, loss, and death in the undergraduate courses she taught or her graduate assistantship, and the synergy between her personal experience and professional expertise was evident in her decision to complement the textbook material by telling her personal story of bereavement in class. Gillian described this teaching opportunity as something that felt "very natural" and "right." Her self-transcendent objectives are apparent in her description of her students' reaction:

> They hear me, and it makes a difference. You know, you feel it makes a difference 'cause every other time they're text-messaging and sleeping. *[laughing]* You know, ...[my story] made a difference to them. I mean, it's just that's why I'm here. That's *totally* why I'm here. Completely why, you know?

Gillian's declaration that teaching about bereavement is "totally why I'm here" was echoed in the way she framed her experience of presenting some autoethnographic[3] research at the ADEC conference.

[3]Autoethnography is a form of social science research where the researcher himself or herself is the primary research subject, or at minimum one of the primary subjects in a study.

She described the process of giving her presentation—a personal reflection supported by scholarly research—as something that she "loved" and was "amazing" that was also "terrifying" and "really, really, really hard." The juxtaposition of love and terror can be seen in Gillian's description of her feelings in the hour leading up to her talk:

> I remember sitting, like, on a chair…and I was *crying*. I was by myself …I'm not very good about displaying my emotions in public… I didn't want to come across as kind of an emotional basket case…especially when I knew I was going to have to get up and talk. I mean I was like, "*How* am I going to do this?…I couldn't even sit through anybody else's [presentation]. How am I supposed to get up and talk about mine to doctors and professors?"

Gillian ultimately decided to go through with the talk. She describes the source of her motivation below:

> This man I'd never met before… came and sat down and he was like, "So, you know, how's it goin'?" [*laughing*] I hadn't met anybody that entire week, and in that moment, like…it's just that feeling, you know? Timothy had something to do with that. And I sat and talked to him for like a good 45 minutes before [my presentation], and I went over my stuff with him and I showed him pictures of Timothy. He was a grief counselor from Canada. It couldn't have been better. I still keep in touch with him…yeah, it was just one of those kind of meant to be kind of feelings.

Despite the fact that even an hour prior to her presentation she "didn't want to do it," Gillian believed that the conference was "one of the best things that…happened" in the past year:

> Walking away from that conference like I *know* where I am. This is *exactly* where I'm supposed to be. This is exactly what I'm supposed to be doing. This is exactly where I'm supposed to be.

In light of the difficult ADEC experience, I asked Gillian if anyone had expressed concern that studying parental bereavement in graduate school would be too difficult emotionally. She acknowledged that "a lot of people" in her family were concerned that the process would be "too much" for her to take and that it would be "emotionally… too hard." Her family questioned why she would want to "constantly put myself into something that's so painful for me to deal with anyway. Like, why would I want to write about, and teach about, something that was the most painful thing I've ever gone through?" Gillian told me that she didn't usually respond directly to these concerns when people voiced them; she knew that they meant well, and they "just don't want to see me hurting." Internally, however, she acknowledged that she felt "frustration" at their comments. Clearly, there were aspects of graduate school that hurt, for instance writing papers near the anniversary of her son's death or speaking about bereavement at professional conferences. Yet, when I asked Gillian if she was sure she was doing the right thing, she replied, "Yeah. Definitely. I don't think I've been more sure of anything in my life, actually."

Gillian Inside the "Well-Lit, Warm Room"

One way to interpret Gillian's graduate school goals of researching and teaching about parental bereavement is to use the metaphor of Frankl's platform in the "well-lit, warm and pleasant lecture room" after the war. It seemed to me that through her goals of writing and teaching about parental bereavement, Gillian, like Frankl, was envisioning a future place of comfort in the midst of her own tragedy. I asked Gillian to read Frankl's vision of educating others about the psychology of the concentration camp (reproduced for readers in Chapter 1) and to tell me if she saw parallels between her work and the goal that helped to save Frankl's life during his imprisonment. When Gillian was still in graduate school, she wholeheartedly endorsed the comparison. Her response follows:

> Definitely. Definitely. I mean, especially this last sentence: "Emotion, which is suffering, ceases to be suffering as soon as we form a clear and precise picture of it (Frankl 1946/2014, p. 69)." It's very true…You can sit and spin [about] what it feels like to lose a child. [*crying*] Every day I think about Timothy and my loss. But as soon as I write it down it becomes very real, but it's out of my head. And it's on paper. And it serves a purpose of becoming something. Everything that I'm feeling and the pain and all of that, it has a *purpose* once it becomes something *real*, you know, *tangible* for somebody else, whether it's my writing or whether I'm getting up and giving a lecture or I have a story or something. Timothy becomes real and…he's not forgotten….it's hard to explain because it is

> so personal…I'm the one stuck with my thoughts and I'm the one thinking about it every day. Instead of just having it kind of go to waste, almost. Like those emotions are just sitting there, and you're thinking them and feeling them. And there's almost some relief in knowing that you're gonna take that and put it into something that's going to be powerful for something else. All of this suffering and all of this pain—I can give it purpose that way. Just because I'm hurting—I can do something good with it…It's a powerful, painful thought. If I don't share it, it will go to waste because it's just in my head. [If] I write it down, I share it…it becomes alive and it's real and it has a purpose.

To illustrate the substantive positive "purpose" Gillian had discovered for her painful thoughts, she told me about the day Timothy died.

> A perfect example is [the] dogwood tree outside my door…we planted [it] the day Timothy died …So that tree to me, it represents that day that we buried my son. It represents my family coming together and burying this tree for Timothy. But every spring when I watch it bloom it reminds me of another year without Timothy. Every time it gets taller, it's like there's more time without Timothy. It's such a powerful thought to have in your head, and to think it and to see it. But when you write it down, and I share it with you, or I…talk about it in lecture it becomes very real. It becomes alive. It becomes very symbolic of what it's like to you know, live without a child. So yeah, I mean I get that. Like, the "Emotion, which is suffering, ceases to be suffering as soon as we form a clear and precise picture of it (Frankl 1946/2014, p. 69)." That's a perfect example of that for me. [It's] very painful for me to watch that [tree] every year…but when I can share it, or I can explain it, or I can give it to somebody else then it doesn't hurt so much. And it has a purpose. That thought has a purpose. It has some symbolic reference to me which another parent would get, or it helps me to explain to somebody else what it feels like.

Gillian also expressed a sense of responsibility toward her grief, and this echoed Frankl's realization that as a psychologist in a concentration camp, he was in a unique position to accomplish something perhaps no one else could:

> You take what you have when you are given it, and you may not have wanted it. I didn't want this. I don't want this. I still don't want it. But I have it. So I've got to use it for something, and if this is the only way

> I've got, I know how to do it....I know that even ten years down the road when I still have these thoughts I can still use them because they're real. They're what I feel. Maybe they'll help explain something else to somebody someday. And it doesn't hurt so much once you get it out there. [*crying, and a little laugh*]

Gillian Ten Years Later

Ten years ago, Gillian told me that after graduation she wanted to become a professor of family studies. In this capacity, she would teach about death, dying, and parental bereavement and publish books and journal articles on these topics. It was also important for her to give presentations for other professionals at conferences. If her voice could be "heard" in these capacities, then laypersons and professionals working with bereaved parents would treat clients more sensitively and effectively than she had been treated. At that time, she foresaw the ongoing value of both her academic training in graduate school and the personal anguish that fueled it. She predicted, "even ten years down the road when I still have these thoughts I can still use them because they're real." However, her situation ten years later looked quite different from what she predicted.

Gillian's career took a surprising turn immediately after graduation. Just as she was finishing her degree, she was presented with an opportunity to apply for a post-doctoral fellowship at an Ivy League university. The position fit her research skill set perfectly. She would be required to work in the educational technology laboratory, but she would also have time to pursue her own research on bereavement. She got the job and moved her family across country for this exciting adventure. Her new laboratory director was very supportive of her bereavement work and connected her with other researchers with similar interests at the university. While pursuing these leads, Gillian presented her dissertation findings locally and wrote a grant for prestigious early career award that would help establish her as a leader in the bereavement field. But she never sent the proposal. As Gillian put it, "I just *stopped.*"

If funded, the grant would have required a five-year commitment, and the research done during that time would likely determine the direction of her research from that point on. Despite having spent four years in graduate school pursuing this goal, Gillian decided she no longer wanted to study bereavement:

> I just—*I couldn't do it. I couldn't.* It's just too much. [*little laugh*] It just got to a point where it was just too much.

Instead, Gillian opted to focus exclusively on the educational technology development and evaluation taking place in the laboratory. She describes the reason for her decision below:

> The educational technology research is *fun*...There's nothing *sad* about it. There's nothing that's *painful* about it. But I remember not submitting that grant, and almost having a sense of *relief* about it....It's exhausting. I really didn't realize how exhausting [bereavement] research is, because it's so personal and painful. And it's people. And it's people that are hurting in a very painful, deep way. And it's emotionally exhausting even if it's not you. It was just emotionally exhausting. When I had the chance to put my feet in some different waters and play around with something creative like educational technology research, and then to put my feet back into the grief and loss research, and realizing how emotional and draining and painful it was. And then I realized I like this water much better. It really was a sense of relief. [*sigh*] I *feel* better. You just get to a point where it's just so *heavy* all the time...I was tired of feeling that heavy. You know, because I enjoyed the educational technology part. It was fun. It's not *painful*.

Looking forward, her professional goals were now focused on advancing educational technology research. It was still of utmost importance to conduct scholarship that was "meaningful and impactful and [would] touch people." But this did not necessarily mean revisiting sensitive areas. She had one idea for a project that would combine her educational technology focus with heart health education, but she was in no hurry to pursue it. In her position of Deputy Director in the technology laboratory, there was no mandate to revisit her torment on a daily basis. And she wanted to keep it that way.

Given this dramatic change in perspective, I asked Gillian if, knowing what she knows now, she would still make the choice to study bereavement in graduate school. She acknowledged that she was glad that she had earned a Ph.D. and that she probably would not have gone back to school in the first place had it not been for her interest in bereavement. However, given the choice she would not study this again. Instead, she might opt for something like computer science, which was more closely related to her current educational technology focus:

> Ugh. Looking back, I couldn't do it again. Yeah. [*little laugh*] *There's no way.* I don't think I would want to. It was just so damn painful! I don't think I would want to do it again…I guess it's in this place that I don't go anymore.

Gillian's unwillingness to revisit that "place" is evidenced by her reluctance to participate in member checking for the present book. In 2008, I wrote a chapter about Gillian for my own dissertation research. As part of this process, she read my drafts and provided a short statement endorsing the final work as a faithful portrayal of her experience in graduate school. Prior to meeting with Gillian in 2017, I sent her copy of that original dissertation chapter and invited her to read it again so she could provide some longitudinal perspective. She could not bring herself to do it. She explained below:

> I started reading it, the first maybe half a page, and I couldn't do it. I think I was more nervous just about what it was going to have in it. You know 'cause when I read that kind of stuff it's still emotional. I just wasn't it a place where I felt like I wanted to feel the feelings. So I was just like, I'll put this away and read it before you come. And even this morning [right before the interview] I was going to do it, but I couldn't put myself in a place where I wanted to feel the feelings. So I didn't. I didn't. I was scared it was going to have stuff in there about Timothy. [*lightly crying*]

I also offered Gillian the opportunity to read the present chapter, but understandably, and for the same reasons, she declined. Recall that some of Gillian's family members had been concerned when she enrolled in graduate school that the experience would be "too much" or "emotionally…too hard" for her. At the time, she found this negativity frustrating, and she pushed onward toward her goals anyway. However, in hindsight she acknowledged the wisdom of proceeding with caution. When I asked Gillian recently if she had any advice for graduate students who were considering studying something personally painful, her recommendations echoed the advice she had rejected more than a decade ago. First, she warned researchers to be absolutely sure they want to build a career on their topic after graduate school. Although she was able to switch to a new focus, this opportunity is exceedingly rare. And it would be very hard to shift back:

> You *can* shift. But sometimes when you shift and you start getting into it, it's hard to shift back, or shift into a new direction. So try to make sure it's what you want to do. I don't know if I could have done grief and loss after having stepped out of it, and been able to peek back in. Because it was relief to step out of it.

Second, she warned of the unexpected emotional toll of seemingly innocuous class assignments in graduate school:

> You're going to have these assignments where it's *not* going to be as hard for someone else to do. 'Cause I remember having to write these things, like, "Why are you passionate about your research?" Okay let me sit down and *ball* for three hours while I type this out. And then I'm going to read it to a bunch of people that I don't know in my class, and I'm going to probably cry when I'm saying it…So you have to just maybe realize that it's going to be constant therapeutic work every day for *years*…things that maybe wouldn't be as emotional to other people—[*little laugh*] Like, simple assignments, of "Why are you interested in the research you're interested in?" could be could painful stuff to do. It could also be very, very therapeutic too, to do, but it could also be very, very painful. So I guess, be prepared for that.

She also counseled that it may be difficult to step away from the pain when your academic reputation is at stake:

> It's going to be hard to take a break when school doesn't take a break. If you've got a paper that's due, and you just can't for the life of you sit down and write it because it's the anniversary of the death of your son—You know, I was really lucky to have the support that I had, but you may not have a professor that is okay with that. You may find that there are times when you just can't sit down and do it, for whatever reason. So I guess maybe be prepared that this will happen, most likely.

Despite these caveats, Gillian remains cautiously supportive of students' decisions to pursue scholarship related to personal pain:

> I guess if you have the passion and the drive to do it, and to keep it up, then yeah, by all means. But I don't think I realized how emotionally exhausting it was until I stepped out of it. It's really exhausting and draining. And I remember this with my dissertation in grad school—There are

> certain times of the year when you *just can't work*. You can't work because it's his birthday, or it's the holidays, or something happened on the news, or you read something, some research that was just emotionally so draining that you have to step away…Can you imagine having a whole entire career of, "I just don't want to do it right now? I don't want to feel this. I don't want to think about this." When it's something a little safer, when there's emotional distance it's easier to work. I guess maybe the lines were very blurry between where work and personal life—I mean, my career is still very much my life, but it doesn't just drain me the way it probably still would.

Meaningful Experiences, in Retrospect

Ten years on, I wanted to know what Gillian remembered as having been meaningful experiences in graduate school. The metaphor of getting her "voice heard" through her research, speaking, and teaching about bereavement had been very important to Gillian in those days. She recalled the passion she felt for this:

> That's where the meaning is…It becomes very personal. I *really* remember wanting to fix things, or help other people…The only way I felt that I could do that is if I had a degree behind my name, and I had some sort of backing, some kind of a stamp that said, "Listen to her, because she has a Ph.D." Wanting the credibility to make people *hear*, because you're trying to be a voice for so many other people that maybe couldn't do that.

I asked her if in the intervening years she had been able to get her voice heard, and if so, what that looked like. She stated that she found achieving this goal to be much more difficult than expected and not just for the emotional reasons cited earlier. Some fields develop quicker than others, and educational technology advances quickly. Bereavement research, it turns out, does not:

> It's just not something that's going to shift very easily. I think it's just a social norm, it's a cultural norm, that when people go though these kind of things, it makes other people uncomfortable. They don't really want to talk to you about it. They can't relate to you very well about it. [*crying*]… I think at a point I just gave up trying to get people to change…I don't know if it's anything you can shift or change. I don't know if I came to any conclusion, looking back, if I shifted anything at all. Which is a pity.

Gillian also told me that she is still an active part of an online bereavement community, and the posts on this page reflect the unchanging nature of the grief experience:

> I'm still a part of the Compassionate Friends…It's a Facebook group for parents who have lost children…I'm still on that every day. New parents [are] coming in all the time, like, "My son just died", or "My daughter died", or "It's the three year anniversary", "It's the 20 year anniversary", "I don't know how to get through this", "I don't want to live". You know, it's all the things I felt. It's all of it. And it's one month later, it's 10 years later. It's all still the same. I guess my hope of being able to make much more of a difference—I don't—Maybe *can't*.

In contrast, it is easy for Gillian to see the impact she's having on the educational technology field:

> Technology moves forward, and you can see it move, and you can make changes, and you can make an impact. We're moving the field because we're advancing research. Death and dying and grief and loss. I don't know how much more there is to advance. It is what it is, is kind of my conclusion… Staying on the cutting edge, and doing new stuff, and feeling like you're adding to the field is really awesome. And it's really quick and fast when it's educational technology because it's shifting and changing so quickly. Death and dying and grief and loss has been around forever. [*laughing*] The research in the field moves very slowly. So in terms of feeling like you're adding to the field—it doesn't feel as rich. It doesn't feel as impactful. You don't see it as immediate, either.

Even with the dramatic change in her career trajectory—and with the caveat that she would never, ever, do it again—Gillian believes that studying bereavement in graduate school was, overall, a therapeutic experience. As she put it, "I know that sounds strange, but it was powerful in the sense of the *therapy* of it." She is particularly grateful that it provided a chance to meet some of the emotional needs she wasn't getting elsewhere:

> You know, that was pretty invaluable, especially since I wasn't getting the support from family and friends, and I wasn't getting what I needed socially…I had to find it elsewhere, and that's where I found it, was the support of research, oddly enough.

Specifically, the research validated that what she was feeling was normal:

> There is a lot of comfort in science. Just because it overrules what people try to say. Like [a particular relative] telling me that we shouldn't talk about it anymore. He just doesn't like to talk about it. We need to move on, you know. He doesn't really like to talk about Timothy at all. He hasn't for a long time. But to know that he's kind of wrong there…And had I not had the school experience with all the work I put into that, then maybe I wouldn't have been strong enough to be like, "He's wrong."

Given that Gillian characterized her graduate school experience as being "therapeutic" and in light of her career changes, I asked her, "would it be fair to say that you got what you needed out of grad school, and then you closed that chapter?" Here is her reply:

> Maybe in some ways, but in a lot of personal ways, no. No. Because it didn't fix it. It didn't make it stop…Life is good, and life is fine and happy and stuff, but it doesn't mean that it makes it all okay. And maybe I was kind of hoping that [graduate school] would have done it, you know. There would have been some sort of greater purpose and meaning in all of it. But…It didn't happen.

She also worried that, in changing research fields, she disappointed her dissertation Chair. When I interviewed Gillian years ago, it was clear that her relationship with this mentor helped her be successful in pursuing such an emotionally salient research area. Graduate school places extraordinary emotional demands even on typical students with relatively impersonal research agendas. In Gillian's case, these demands were compounded exponentially. She needed a supportive relationship with a professional ally. As Gillian put it eleven years ago, "I'd be lost without her." Professionally, this mentor had been a role model who Gillian described as being "exactly where" she wanted to be eventually. Gillian also sought her approval. When I asked her directly if she could think of a defining moment where she knew she should be researching and writing about parental bereavement, she told me how her mentor thought certain papers were publishable and encouraged her to pursue the Ph.D. The bottom line for Gillian was, "She believes in me." Ten years later, Gillian was troubled by the thought that her change in direction had disappointed this "phenomenal" scholar. In addition to becoming such an important source of support and encouragement personally, Gillian believed her dissertation Chair had always viewed her as the heir to an intellectual legacy. The field studying bereavement is small, so there are not a lot of people to fill the role she abandoned.

Despite her decision to pursue other research areas, Gillian's personal loss tethers her to the bereavement field. One positive legacy of her graduate school experience is that feels well-equipped too advocate for grieving parents when she encounters them. Her status as a bereaved mother gives her empathy, but her Ph.D. gives her courage:

> I feel very much like an advocate, and very strong in the sense of when I see others going through [grief], I have no problem standing up and saying—I'm very confident in, like, "It's okay that you feel this way." Or "I kind of understand how you feel." I guess there's a lot of validation because I dug so deep into the research about it.

Gillian Outside the "Well-Lit, Warm Room," Ten Years Later

When Gillian was in graduate school, the metaphor of Frankl's "well-lit, warm and pleasant lecture room" seemed an apt metaphor for her experience, and she was able to articulate with great clarity her resonance with Frankl's vision. Ten years later, I invited her to read Frankl's description again. Sobered by experience and wiser from her decade in the academy, she was no longer willing to endorse the connection:

> "Emotion, which is suffering, ceases to be suffering as soon as we form a clear and precise picture of it (Frankl 1946/2014, p. 69)." I don't know if I agree with that. I don't know if [*big sigh*] it's that easy, that we can just remove ourselves and look at it, recognize it, pull ourselves out and look into it, and say, "I can see it as something in the past". Maybe I just can't detach yet. Maybe one day it will feel that way, but at the same time, too, I can remember being in places...of having to, [say] "Okay, I've gotta get up, and I've gotta brush my teeth, and then I've gotta do this." And being able to only think sometimes, a few minutes and a few hours ahead, just to get through a day or a week. I remember thinking that way, and trying to figure out how I was going to get through the next week or month or two months or whatever. So I understand how to feel that way, and I also understand how kind of step out and look back

> and be like, holy shit, that was a really bad place. But I don't know if I agree—It doesn't cease to feel like suffering as soon as we're able to kind of step out of it. At least not for me, anyway. I mean I wish it was that easy! [*laughing*] I mean I wish—I *wish* it were that easy, that you could just put your brain into a different place. Because I don't think that's realistic for anybody.

Conclusions

Whether or not Gillian ended up on Frankl's metaphorical platform in a well-lit, warm room, it is clear from the data that (1) the work she did in graduate school served therapeutic aims, and (2) her bereavement scholarship utilized both her academic training and her insider understanding of the target phenomena. She recognized her unique position as a social scientist/sufferer and felt a sense of responsibility to use this double consciousness make her voice "heard." In doing so, she manifested her self-transcendent goal of helping other bereaved parents who did not have the specialized academic training. The meaning Gillian derived from her scholarship motivated her to continue this work for four years even when she found it "terrifying" and "absolutely draining" emotionally. When she finished this important work, she moved to a different place, both geographically and psychologically. She is now focusing new, more joyful goals.

In the years since graduate school, Gillian's life had taken many pleasant and surprising turns. Recently remarried to a handsome young colleague, she is happy to be studying something radically different from what she had set out to do. Her all-consuming focus on understanding and communicating research on parental bereavement had been replaced by the brightness and creativity of her new academic role, and by delight in the recent changes to her family. She described the resulting shift in her perspective:

> I was so focused… during my Ph.D., [but] this whole other part of my life has happened. I met somebody, and I got married, and he has a daughter, so I have a new daughter! That trumps all the other stuff. I was so driven before…and then life throws you a Curve ball and you realize there's so much more to life…I think having a partner… that kind of trumps a lot of it, too. So maybe I haven't…made a lot of waves like I had planned to, but maybe they're still to come. Maybe I'm still going to do something.

As we neared the end of our interview, I suggested to Gillian that perhaps she had already done enough. Besides, despite her overwhelming reluctance to revisit that "place" of grief, she was willing to share her story with me once again. How heroic. People will read about her in this book—you are reading about her now—and in this way, her voice is still being "heard." She acknowledged this as true. At that point, our discussion turned to some of the fun things she was working on in her laboratory. We drove back to her house, where her daughter and her new husband were waiting to welcome her home.

Gillian's Advice for Graduate Students Considering Unusually Personal Scholarship

- If you have the passion and the drive to engage in scholarship related to an area that is painful for you personally, consider doing it. It can be profoundly therapeutic.
- Weigh your options. If you want to get a Ph.D., consider studying something "lighter." If you choose the more personal path, there is no getting away from it. You will be confronting your pain every day. For years.
- It can be hard to change research topics mid-career. If you choose to stay in academia, you may be studying this topic for rest of your life.
- Class discussions and breezy "get to know you" assignments that are easy and fun for others may be very difficult for you. You will constantly be invited to tell strangers why you chose your research topic.
- You will not just be writing about your research. You will also be expected to give presentations. This will make you feel vulnerable. Can you talk formally about your research without breaking down?
- There may be times during the year when *you just can't work* (e.g., the anniversary of your loss, the holidays). You may need to get extensions for assignments. If possible, talk to your professors in advance. Recognize the impact that this may have on your timeline, or on how others view you.
- Grad school can be an isolating experience for students who are carrying a heavy burden. You may not feel understood by your classmates. Make sure you have a supportive mentor on campus.

Gillian's Dissertation Chair's Advice for Mentors and Senior Colleagues

- Understand that conducting research—especially qualitative research—can be emotionally overwhelming for some students even when the topic is unrelated to suffering or loss. This is because deep engagement with the subject is inherent in quality work.
- Each student is unique and will require a different focus of your energy. There is no consistent protocol for advising students with unusually personal connections to their scholarship.
- Mentors and senior colleagues should begin by reflecting on their own ability to advise a student researching a topic that they (the advisor) may find emotionally overwhelming. Are you cut out for this? Will your own "baggage" get in the way?
- When holding initial meetings with students, try to get a sense of their emotional readiness to do the work they are proposing. Gillian's loss was profound. Someone else might have been overwhelmed, but Gillian had the inner strength, sense of mission, and coping methods to carry her through and beyond.
- Dissertation work can be lonely, and this can stifle progress. Facilitate a sense of community by holding regular student get-togethers at your home or another pleasant venue. The students can support each other when they are struggling.
- Consider asking students to prepare by reading about the role of emotions in qualitative work.
- Encourage students to keep journals about their studies. This can include the mechanics of the study (theoretical foundation, methodology, data analysis, writing challenges, etc.).
- More importantly, these journal entries should demonstrate an ongoing assessment of themselves as the principal research instrument.

References

Bourdieu, P., & Passeron, J.-C. (1986). The forms of capital. In J. G. Richardson (Ed.), *Handbook for theory and research for the sociology of education* (pp. 241–258). Santa Barbara, CA: Greenwood.

Du Bois, W. E. B. (1887, August). Strivings of the Negro people. *The Atlantic*, p. 197.

Du Bois, W. E. B. (1903/1994). *The souls of black folk*. New York: Dover.

Frankl, V. E. (1946/2014). *Man's search for meaning*. Boston: Beacon Press.

Kübler-Ross, E. (1969). *On death and dying*. New York: Routledge.

Reed-Danahay, D. E. (Ed.). (1997). *Auto/ethnography: Rewriting the self and the social*. New York: Berg.

CHAPTER 3

Social Sciences: Coming Out as a Scholar Activist

Jesse	*Every single time I'd do a talk in grad school it was a struggle when it got to the point when I would say, "I'm a transgender person. Let me tell you my story." Now I love doing it. I love talking about it. We had a lot of interaction about, "Why did you do this if it's so painful?" "Because I don't have a choice" is about all I could articulate. Well now I can say the reason that I had to do it is that I knew on some level it would get me here.*
Amber	*And here is?*
Jesse	*Where I'm comfortable and love to talk about it. I mean, this is who I was trying to become. I just didn't know it.*

—Jesse, Gender Identity Scholar and Activist, 2017

I am so excited to see Jesse again. Unlike the other participants in this study, Jesse is a dear friend who began and ended graduate school the same year as I. If you are reading this book, we probably have some similar experiences and you know how hazing rituals like statistics courses and prepping for qualifying exams can bond people. Of course, studying the experiences of someone with whom you have another relationship presents ethical challenges. Thankfully, there is an ever-increasing body of literature available to help researchers who are interested in working across these boundaries (e.g., Ellis 2004, 2007; Fine 1994; Owton and Allen-Collinson 2013; Tillmann-Healy 2001, 2003).

Jesse is a transgender person. He is biologically female, and he self-identifies as a male. He does not attempt to pass as a biological male;

A. Esping, *Epistemology, Ethics, and Meaning in Unusually Personal Scholarship*, https://doi.org/10.1007/978-3-319-73718-8_3

people who meet Jesse see a masculine female body wearing masculine or gender-neutral clothing. He is gracious about pronouns, preferring "he," but understanding that it takes time for some people to make the mental shift. Jesse teaches statistics at an R1 university and also travels nationally giving talks about gender development that combines biological science (e.g., there are more intersexed people[1] than there are people born with cystic fibrosis) (Intersex Society of North America 2008), social science (e.g., sexual orientation and gender identity are not the same thing) (American Psychological Association 2015), and his own personal experience growing up as a transgender person. He is paid handsomely for these talks, which often take place at universities, and he has won numerous awards for this work. He has also been featured in a documentary and on television. In pretty much every other way, Jesse lives an ordinary life. At 56, he lives in a picturesque country house with his wife, Liz, a big fluffy dog, and a strawberry garden. He has talents in a variety of creative endeavors, including art and music, and I have often thought of him as somewhat of a Renaissance man.

Transgender individuals like Jesse do not identify with the sex that they were assigned at birth (American Psychological Association 2015). Jesse was born with a female body, but this never felt right to him. His first conscious memories of feeling male can be traced to his preschool years, although his parents told him that he felt this much earlier. When Jesse was very young, he liked to play with toys that were typically associated with boys, and he was attracted to boys' games. The fundamental thing, however, was that Jesse wanted to *be* a boy. At least that is how his preschool mind could conceptualize it. The truth is, Jesse knew that on some level, he really *was* a boy. When he voiced this desire, his mother responded in a threatening way:

> I remember my mother taking me aside…and saying "You don't really want to be a boy, do you? You just like playing with boys toys." And I said "No. I want to be a boy." And she said "Well, that's not okay. It's okay if you just like playing with boys' stuff, but if you really want to be a boy

[1]The term "intersex" is often used to describe a person who is born with "reproductive or sexual anatomy that doesn't seem to fit the typical definitions of female or male." There are many intersex conditions. Examples include a baby born with some cells that are XX and some that are XY, or an infant with genitals exhibiting both typically "male" and typically "female" characteristics (Intersex Society of North America 2008).

> then I've gotta do something about that... I'm gonna have to take all our toys away from you, and you're gonna start playing with dolls and dishes... And you'll have to wear dresses and skirts all the time. And we're gonna have to let your hair grow and start fixing it up and making you okay with [being] a girl. Now you don't really [want to be] a boy, do you?" And I said "no" because I didn't want all that stuff to happen.

Jesse learned two things from his mother's response. First, he learned that there must be something "intrinsically flawed" and "wrong" with him because he wanted to be a boy. Second, he learned that it was not safe to talk about wanting to be a boy—even to himself. He stopped stating this desire to others and eventually stopped acknowledging it inside his own mind. It became quite literally "unthinkable." Nevertheless, Jesse remained a male child inside a female body. Schoolmates taunted him; for example, Jesse recalled someone signing his yearbook, "to a nice boy/girl." Adults also made their disapproval apparent by shaking their heads and speaking to each other in loud whispers as if he couldn't hear them. Clucking their tongues, they said things like, "That Jesse...She's just not what you'd expect from a girl." Jesse didn't feel that he was *doing* anything to warrant this treatment: It was just who I was...And people *knew* that what I was—was different.

The Transgender "Epiphany"

Jesse had his first romantic relationship with a female partner shortly after he graduated from college. At the age of 21, he came out as a gay woman. At age 27, he met his partner (now wife) Liz, and for many years, he considered himself one female half of a lesbian couple. However, in his early forties he had an "epiphany" that he was not gay, but was in fact a transgender man.

For several months prior to this revelation, Jesse had been feeling depressed, anxious, and overly self-critical. He and his therapist spent several weeks exploring possible causes for his distress, but nothing specific emerged. In the quote below, Jesse explains the moment when he figured it all out:

> [My dog] and I went out into the woods...probably for two or three hours...and I just was really racking my brain trying to figure this out. And I couldn't...come up with anything... And *finally* I just said "I just gotta

> quit. Because, I can't do this on my own" ...Liz and I had a potluck to go to...I had just enough time to get back home, shower and go meet her there...I was very task-oriented at that point. I was just getting ready, not really thinking about anything. I had showered and I had dressed and I'm sitting on the bed, leaning over tying my shoes. And I heard this *voice*. It just *hit* me upside the head, like someone hit me with a baseball bat. I heard this voice in my head. It was a male voice, but it was *my* voice. It was my voice and it was male. And it said, "I don't feel like a woman." And I mean I just—I just *stopped*. I mean I was in mid *[demonstrates tying shoes]* and I just *stopped*...And in that instant *[sigh]* I got inundated with all of these memories. Memories of not feeling female. All my life. Specific... instances where...peers that I grew up with had problems with me and teased me about being different. Masculine. Memories of adults shaking their head and saying things about me as if I couldn't hear them...I remembered...things like how *painful* it was not to be able to play little league... every memory...had an emotion attached to it. I not only re-lived the incident, I re-lived the emotional response... I probably spent a good 45 min [experiencing] just one memory after the other...It was *so* powerful.

Jesse repeatedly characterized this moment as an "epiphany." Very early in life, he had internalized the judgment that it was "not okay" and "wrong" to want to be a boy. Out of self-protection, he had gone into denial, and for nearly 40 years, he had kept an "unthinkable" secret from everyone, including himself. This had caused Jesse a great deal of suffering, which was compounded by the disapproval and outright cruelty of a world that is often hostile to people Jesse later came to refer to in his academic work as the "atypically gendered." Reconnecting with his male identity provided some relief, but it also involved new psychological discomfort; Jesse described his personal experience of coming out as gay in his early twenties as "a piece of cake" as compared with the emotional consequences of realizing he was transgender in midlife.

Graduate School

Jesse's transgender epiphany coincided with a career crisis. He enjoyed the artistic work he had been doing, but this was becoming increasingly more difficult physically. He had long known that he would need to transition into something else, but had been unclear what this something else should be. After some deliberation and consultation with Liz and his therapist, he came to the realization, "I need to study gender." If all went well, this would eventually lead to a faculty position at a university. Jesse was attracted to this idea for both personal and professional reasons. From a personal standpoint, he believed that studying gender in graduate school would provide a chance to "work my own issue." The intellectual opportunities promised by the academic environment suited Jesse's analytical mind:

> I intellectualize a lot anyway. *[sigh]* Liz and I are very different this way. When she goes to therapy, she goes to therapy to cry and to emote and to beat up a pillow, get her emotions out...And I go to therapy to *talk*. I want to figure it out. I want to *break* it down. I want to make *sense* out of it...Which is why grad school is a fit for me...I've *been* emotional with this. I've spent *hours* crying in therapy and you know...I haven't hidden from that. But I [also] have to *analyze* it.

From a professional standpoint, Jesse believed that he could do research that "needed to be done." He liked the idea of conducting studies that would call into question the veracity of the "two-and-only-two-sex/two-gender paradigm." He thought society's commitment to the "erroneous" belief that sex and gender are dichotomous contributed to robbing boys of the tools to deal with emotional distress, and took away girls' assertiveness and independence. He also believed the paradigm was at least partly responsible for homophobia and heterosexism. Perhaps in graduate school, he could contribute something that would help create positive change.

Choice and Evolution of a Dissertation Topic: The Research-Interest Closet

Jesse ultimately spent a great deal of time during his Ph.D. program teaching and writing about transgenderism. However, the term "transgender" did not appear in the statement of purpose he wrote for his application to graduate school. In the first paragraph, he discussed the incidence of violent behavior against homosexuals. He followed by stating several broad questions about gender:

> Why are people so committed to prescribed gender roles? Why does gender non-adherence elicit responses in people that range from disgust to

> violent contempt? Where did traditional gender roles come from in the first place and what specifically are they? What exactly is gender? And "What, beyond our anatomy, makes us women and men?" Are the two categories, men & women, mutually exclusive…?

Six years later, I asked Jesse to provide me with a copy of this document. When he sent it, he also sent a clarifying email:

> When I wrote that essay I was just a few months away from the "trans epiphany". [I] was nowhere near ready to get "out of the closet"…[and was] feeling overwhelmed at the prospect of going back to school after almost 20 years, [and] questioning whether I was going to be good enough to get through a doctoral program, and [was] generally not in a good psychological space…Consequently, I wasn't using the term "transgender" in my application at all, which was a conscious choice. It would be a misinterpretation to think that I evolved into studying trans issues; I went to school to study transgenderism. I just wasn't saying so directly at the time.

In his personal life, Jesse was not yet "out" as a transgender person, and this discretion was echoed in his decision not to be "out" professionally as a researcher interested in studying transgenderism. He didn't know how the admissions committee would respond to him if he was completely honest about his motivations; even admitting he was interested *intellectually* in transgenderism felt dangerous. From both personal and professional perspectives, talking obliquely about homosexuality and gender roles was "safer." Jesse had spent his whole life trying to fit in, most of the time unsuccessfully. He was not going to risk rejection once again.

When Jesse entered the Ph.D. program, he did not yet have the methodological sophistication as a researcher to know how to attack the two-and-only-two-sex/two-gender paradigm empirically, so he was open to exploring tangential research areas. In the meantime, he focused on learning as much as he could about social science[2] and research methods. In his personal life, he kept working at embracing his hard-wrought self-understanding. By his second semester of graduate school, Jesse was feeling much more comfortable with himself as a transgender person. When

[2] I have chosen to use the broad descriptor "social science" to avoid specifying Jesse's academic discipline.

speaking casually to an advanced graduate student about transgenderism, he spontaneously said, "Well, if you hadn't guessed, I'm one of these people." The other student responded positively and immediately asked Jesse if he would be willing to speak to the undergraduate course she was teaching. Jesse agreed, and from this point on, he was open with other graduate students and faculty about his transgender identity. He quickly became well known in the department and beyond as a compelling and highly sought-after guest speaker; in these talks, he provided theoretical and empirical perspectives on sex and gender development. He also shared his own story.

Jesse's new openness with regard to his transgender identity was complemented by his increasing sophistication as a researcher, and by his fourth year of graduate school, he was pursuing a research agenda focused on finding empirical evidence for the inadequacy of the dichotomous sex/gender paradigm. He had discovered a fondness and an aptitude for statistics, and he recognized that quantitative methods could be used in an innovative study to determine how people view the relative importance of various biological factors in determining the sex of ambiguous individuals. One theoretical underpinning of this particular study was that sex and gender are not dichotomous. Jesse believed this line of research could use empirical science to attack the dichotomous sex/gender assumption "at its core." The results could have practical implications for the way society responds to intersexed babies, and by extension other atypically gendered individuals:

> [Intersexed babies] are being reacted to the way they are…because of the way people view gender. It's because [society is saying] "By god, there's male and there's female, and there's nothing [else]. And if you don't fit this then we gotta cut you up until you do, at the expense of everything else. Even if it's a surgery every year until you're 12 years old…It could be the expense of being incontinent or needing to have a catheter on a regular basis because there's so much scar tissue in there. But we're gonna keep cutting you up because by god you don't fit this paradigm"… I'm attacking the problem at its core. And the core is the *two-gender paradigm doesn't fit everybody.*

Jesse believed his dissertation could be a first step toward building a body of research demonstrating the inadequacy of the dichotomous sex/gender paradigm. If he was successful, then other atypically gendered people might experience the sense of belonging and acceptance that he had so longed for as a male child in a female body. This would be healing. Moreover, if his research could move society toward abandoning its reliance on the two-and-only-two-sex/gender assumption, then Jesse's life as a transgender adult might also improve: In his second interview, Jesse elaborated on the personal significance of his proposed dissertation:

> I have been personally hurt and damaged, and my life is *harder* on a daily basis because of the two-gender paradigm. My issues, my insecurities. I mean, a lot of that stuff comes...from the experience of growing up male in a female body...I suffer on a daily [basis]. It's *hard*. It's harder for me to be out in the world than it should be. Because of this paradigm....It's a battle. It's a personal battle, and I'm not alone in it. I'm not the only person who's ever hurt.

Thus, Jesse's goal of helping others held promise for helping himself. Jesse was very excited about this dissertation idea. He pursued it for several months, but he was ultimately forced to abandon it because the person he wanted to chair his dissertation committee did not support his premise that the dichotomous paradigm failed to adequately describe that part of human experience referred to as sex and gender. Jesse removed the uncooperative person from his committee, but he also decided to shift to a less controversial dissertation topic focusing on statistical research methodology as it relates to studying sex and gender. He would wait to attack the dichotomous paradigm more directly after graduation.

Most graduate students placed in the same situation would feel discouraged, so Jesse was not unique in this respect. However, Jesse's personal stake in his research agenda worsened the sting. In graduate school, his professional objectives and his personal identity as an atypically gendered person were closely intertwined. In rejecting Jesse's premise that the dichotomous sex/gender paradigm is erroneous, it felt like the committee member was ultimately rejecting Jesse. This is precisely what had worried him initially when he decided to avoid using the word "transgender" in his statement of purpose many years earlier.

In the end, Jesse grew to genuinely appreciate his final dissertation idea. And his committee agreed that his work was, psychometrically speaking, superb. This helped him land a tenure-track position teaching statistics in a large state school.

Meaningful Experiences in Graduate School

When I interviewed Jesse while he was still in graduate school, I asked him to tell me about some experiences that felt "meaningful" to him. He told me several stories over the course of our three yearly interviews, and I was also able to infer some other meaningful experiences based on the data. Here are two examples.

The Impact of Academic Work on Self-Understanding

Jesse and Gillian are alike in that they both explicitly stated that self-understanding was one reason to study their chosen topics in graduate school. Gillian wanted to learn about "the emotions behind what it meant to be a bereaved parent," and Jesse viewed graduate school as an opportunity to harness his analytical strengths and "work my own issue." One fascinating finding emerging from Jesse's interview data is the degree to which his new academic understanding of human development had become integrated into his personal story of growing up as a transgender person. For example, when Jesse shared with me his very early memory of telling his mother that he wanted to be a boy, he added as an aside that although he firmly believed the recollection to be true, "memories aren't always accurate." He had learned about the fallibility of human memory in one of his courses. Another example of the integration of Jesse's academic work with his personal narrative occurred when he told me about a time when he decided to dress and act like a girl in junior high school. He thought that this would make his classmates stop bullying him. He specifically referenced his adolescent development course when he explained to me the probable reasons for, and outcomes of, this experiment:

> As you know from teaching development and taking [a specific professor's] adolescent development class, early adolescence is a time of gender intensification…Kids adopt *really* stringent gender roles. And I think part of that is…this feeling of "Wow. I'm starting to grow up. I need to be a man. I need to be a woman."

This attempt to fit in as a girl did not work. In fact, it compounded his misery, because now his classmates teased him for trying to look like a girl. The developmental insight picked up from his coursework could not exonerate his peers' actions; it might make the cruelty seem a bit more comprehensible to his adult mind: Kids at that age can be mean, yes. But it is also normal for them to be hyper-focused on gender roles.

The "Gender Talks": Coming Out in a Very Public Way

Recall that when Jesse wrote his statement of purpose for his graduate school application, he was unwilling to risk using the word "transgender." However, by his third semester in graduate school he had come out in a very public way. The first time he told another graduate student about his transgender identity, that student asked him to speak to an undergraduate class she was teaching. He agreed. This decision proved to have profound implications for Jesse's search for meaning in graduate school.

Jesse articulated both personal and professional reasons for doing his gender presentations. Professionally, he viewed them as "activism." In this way, his motivation mirrored his desire to find evidence for the inadequacy of the two-and-only-two-sex/gender paradigm. His presentations, like his research, "needed to be done":

> [Often] people's only exposure to transgenderism are the people they see on *Jerry Springer*.[3] And to see someone who's becoming a professional, becoming a scholar, becoming an academic—who's not a guy in a wig—talk hopefully intelligently about this and then say, "By the way, I am one of these people." I just think that, that really has an opportunity to make a difference in how people think. And one of the reasons I continue to do it is that I have had people stop me… and say "You talked to my class last year or last semester or earlier this semester. And you've *changed* the way I think about gender".

Jesse's delight in the fact that he had changed people's minds through his work in graduate school echoes Gillian's goal of using her scholarship to become "a part of the changing theories and views on bereavement." Jesse was also concretely manifesting Gillian's metaphor of getting one's "voice heard." While Jesse lamented that "people's only exposure to transgenderism are the people they see on *Jerry Springer*," Gillian was

[3] Jerry Springer hosted a sensationalist daytime television show in the 1990s and early 2000s.

troubled that the only thing people typically know about bereavement is Kübler-Ross's (1969) five-stage theory, which she rejected. In both cases, the desire to shift how others view their particular circumstance was an essential and meaningful part of their graduate school experience.

In addition to finding the chance to educate others meaningful, Jesse found his gender talks personally healing. They were a vital part of his coming-out process:

> I've lived my *whole* life hiding this, and I'm not going to do it anymore… [These talks have been] a very therapeutic thing for me…I've lived my whole life being very hidden…and withholding. And not letting people see me because I didn't want to be rejected. Well two things have happened. I've stood up and I've said "This is who and what I am." And I *haven't* been rejected. And the few people who've had a problem with it, I've had to [say] "It doesn't matter. I'm still okay." So it's given me that.

Approximately a year after Jesse said this, he told me he would be giving only one or two-gender presentations during the current semester. In previous semesters, he had presented six to ten times, often to crowds of around 100 people. This was just too much. Moreover, the talks had served their purpose in providing a way to actualize his coming-out process, and he no longer felt the need to do this repeatedly. At this point, he was more focused on his "sense of responsibility" and his "duty to educate" others about atypically gendered individuals. Jesse seemed to recognize that the pain he endured because of his gender conflict could be channeled in a positive direction:

> I don't think I have a need, on a personal level, to do these talks. Now I think I'm still doing it because people need to hear it…I do it because… it's a responsibility. People need to hear this, and I'm uniquely qualified to tell them. Not that I'm the only person in the universe who can do it, but…I *am* in a unique position.

Here we find another similarity to the way Gillian framed her search for meaning in graduate school. In acknowledging his sense of responsibility toward his unique position, Jesse seems to reflect Gillian's sense of "purpose" with regard to her bereavement. Her suffering, she told me, "become[s] something" when she speaks to classes or publishes bereavement research. It does not "go to waste" when she is able to "use it for something" like educating others. One interpretation of this is that both Jesse and Gillian shared the sense of responsibility Frankl articulated with regard to using his unique constellation of personal and academic understandings of suffering to educate others after his liberation. For all three scholars, Gillian, Jesse, and Frankl, this manifested in publications and presentations given in—as Frankl put it—"well-lit, warm and pleasant lecture rooms" (Frankl 1946/2014, p. 68).

Jesse Inside the "Well-Lit, Warm Room"

On two occasions when Jesse was in graduate school, I asked him to read Frankl's quote about speaking in the "well-lit, warm and pleasant lecture room" (reproduced for readers in Chapter 1) and to tell me if he identified with Frankl's vision. Jesse responded by explaining that when he started graduate school, he was primarily focused on learning more about gender, rather than on teaching others about it. That first opportunity to give a gender presentation came about "by accident" when the other graduate student asked him to speak to her class. Before that, he had "never dreamed about giving presentations all over campus." Like Gillian, Jesse took special notice of the excerpt from Frankl's quote, "Emotion, which is suffering, ceases to be suffering as soon as we form a clear and precise picture of it" (Frankl 1946/2014, p. 69). In response, he stated: "I think that's true. I think that's why I go about things intellectually." He also elaborated on the difference between talking intimately with another person about his gender identity and speaking about it publically. He noted that it was harder to speak personally with one professor about his gender identity than it was to give a presentation to a room full of them. Speaking to the group felt "safer":

> There is something very different about standing up in that role, with that persona and talking about this personal stuff that is very different from sitting down one on one and talking about it. And it *does* objectify it.

Jesse also saw his research as a platform. This, too, came as a bit of a surprise. The body of work he expected to learn from in graduate school didn't exist. In choosing to attack the dichotomous two-sex/gender paradigm via statistical analyses of data, rather than philosophically, he was breaking new ground. This was a bit frightening, but it also promised exciting opportunities to contribute something positive to the world:

> I'm not the first person to say that the dichotomy has a problem...but as near as I can tell [I am the first person to attack it statistically]... I didn't know I was going to break [new] ground. I really didn't plan on that... Sometimes it gets really overwhelming ...I'm breaking new ground here. And to go someplace without a roadmap is—You know, the unknown can be frightening. Well, this really is the unknown. But there's another part of me that feels like the zeitgeist is right. I mean it's time for this stuff to come out. *Beyond* the philosophical, and beyond the gender studies world. I think that it's time that it hit mainstream.

Jesse Ten Years Later

It turns out Jesse's prediction was correct. When I met with him at his home ten years later, the word "transgender" had become much more mainstream. In the intervening years, people had come to know celebrities like Chaz Bono and Caitlyn Jenner[4] through their books and frequent media appearances. Although often sensationalized, the press coverage was not quite the *Jerry Springer Show.* People sometimes got their facts wrong, but at least they had a general idea of what "transgender" might mean. As Jesse explained:

> Used to I'd say "transgender" and people didn't even know what I was talking about...I can't believe how much it's changed, and how quickly it's changed...it's just incredible. It didn't change that much during the seven years I was in grad school, but it just really took off. So the zeitgeist is very different.

That's not all that is different. I asked Jesse to read the chapter I wrote about him for my dissertation nearly a decade ago. Unlike Gillian, he was eager to do so. When I asked for his impressions, he responded that reading it recalled to him the "despair" he had been feeling in the years immediately following his transgender "epiphany":

> I had remembered just kind of this general unhappiness, severe unhappiness, at the time, but it was like, oh yeah, this was the real *nature* of what I was feeling at the time...It made me appreciative of how far I've come.

[4] Chaz Bono is the transgender son of Sonny Bono and Cher. Caitlyn Jenner is the trans woman formerly known as Bruce Jenner. Jesse had the opportunity to meet Chaz Bono through his work in this area.

And Jesse had indeed come very far both personally and professionally since graduation. Although he is still attentive to his original goal of attacking the dichotomous two-and-only-two-sex/gender paradigm, in some ways his scholarship has evolved as much as Gillian's did. What has changed for Jesse is not his focus, but rather his reasons for doing it. The progression was immediately evident to him as he was reading my dissertation chapter. He is still doing presentations about gender, but his perspective on their purpose is radically different:

> I noticed that last night when I read it. When you interviewed me last, I wanted to save the world. I wanted to make a difference. I wanted to change people's minds. I knew I couldn't change everyone, but I wanted to change the people who were ready, you know. I want to do this now because I love it. I have fun. And I love every piece of it. I love the travel. I love going in. I have made some really deep friendships that have lasted 12 hours. I may never see these people again, but so what? Meeting these people, *I can't tell you* the conversations I've had with people. "Hey can we go get some coffee?" And it's, "I'm a straight man, but I was never masculine enough. I was never macho enough, so I'm not a typical man in that way." And so they want to tell me their story. Or, "I'm a masculine female. Everybody assumes I'm gay, but I'm not. But yet I never felt comfortable." So straight people often really identify. And all they really want to do is tell me their story. And then I just try to affirm who they are.

The personal fulfillment Jesse gets from these talks has also changed dramatically since graduate school. Back then, coming out during the talks was an excruciating process. Now, it is much more joyful:

Jesse My goal with all of this is to enjoy life. Period. That has become my number one thing. I'm not doing this really for anybody else but me. Now put that in the context of someone who for 40 years could not *speak* what they were. So yeah, now I'm just getting out there in a very public way, saying "this is who I am" and *loving* it while I'm doing it. Now you know that's a shift because you know how much I struggled with coming out. Every single time I'd do a talk in grad school it was a *struggle* when it got to the point when I would say, "I'm a transgender person. Let me tell you my story." Now I love doing it. I love talking about it. We had a lot of interaction about, "Why

	did you do this if it's so painful?" "Because I don't have a choice" is about all I could articulate. Well now I can say the reason that I had to do it is that I knew on some level it would get me here.
Amber	And "here" is?"
Jesse	Where I'm comfortable and love to talk about it. I mean, this is who I was trying to become. I just didn't know it.

Jesse also acknowledged that he is surprisingly detached from the outcomes of these trips:

> I'm not doing it so that people will be able to change or, to you know. People either hear my message or they don't. I'm not attached to that anymore…And it's none of my business how they take it. Even in grad school I had people stop me on campus and say, "Hey, you talked to my class and you changed how I think." Cool! I love it when that happens. I love it when I'm teaching statistics and somebody gets it. But I don't lose sleep when they don't. You know, I'm putting it out there because I want to put it out there. I've always been a public speaker. I always knew how to do that, and I was always pretty good at it. And I love doing it. So I do it because I love it. The fact that it makes a difference is icing on the cake. And I love it, and I appreciate it, but it's not why I do it.

One reason for this shift in perspective may be that Jesse's career since graduate school has not been at all what he wanted or expected. Immediately after graduation, he accepted a position at a large state school with a high (and because of budget cuts, seemingly ever-increasing) teaching load, very little support, and low expectations for faculty research. He knew going in that it was not the ideal fit, but it was local, and staying put would allow his wife to keep her job. However, having just come from an R1 atmosphere, the workload was shocking. Other than "running numbers" for other people's studies, he did not publish. Charged with teaching all of the statistics courses in his college (courses which also serviced other programs in the university), there was simply no time.

When Jesse graduated, he thought he would use his faculty position as a platform to reach the mainstream. Fortunately, his university viewed his gender talks as scholarship, so he was able to start building his national reputation this way. However, thwarted in his attempt to publish scholarly papers, he ultimately realized that the academy might not be the best fit for this goal:

> Professionally I've been doing the talks. I've also been on TV a couple of times…I have always seen really wanted to eventually take this discussion into the mainstream. And I always thought that would be through academe, you know, writing academically and then getting into the mainstream that way. That didn't happen. Maybe that's for the best. Maybe just taking it directly to the mainstream will be the better way to go.

A few years after receiving tenure and being promoted to associate professor at his first institution, Jesse accepted a non-tenure-track position at an R1 university. This new job involves teaching statistics courses, but carries no expectations for research. He is looking forward to having time to write about gender again, but he is unsure if this will take the form of formal academic writing or something geared more toward the public. More important, his new department is excited about his talks and seems very willing to support his travel schedule. He now thinks of himself more as a public speaker and advocate than an academic:

> I'm getting paid as a professional speaker, and that's building and it's growing. And *that* is who I am professionally. Professor, academic, is more of a job title to me than an identity…My professional identity is public speaker and advocate, and I hope to do it full time eventually.

That said, Jesse believes his position at the university gives him a certain amount of credibility to serve this aim:

> I think being connected with the university I'm with now and the department I'm with now—I mean this is the number one school of its kind in the nation right now. So I think that's a credibility that will help me.

Meaningful Experiences, in Retrospect

In light of the many unexpected changes in Jesse's professional life since his graduation, I was eager to learn how he remembered the emotional salience of his graduate school experience. In my dissertation chapter about Jesse, I had been hesitant to label his overall experience as "therapeutic," in part because of the emotional toll of having to change directions with his dissertation (which, incidentally, kept him in school for an extra year). After reading the chapter ten years later, Jesse pointed out my reticence. His response specifically called into question my disinclination to call his graduate school experience by Frankl's, term, "logotherapeutic," which refers to healing through discovering meaning in suffering (Frankl 1946/2014):

Jesse	That's another thing I wanted to say. You had drawn a conclusion that because of A, B, and C, my graduate school experience was not logotherapeutic…however there were elements of that, you know? I've read some Frankl, but I'm not the expert you are, so I can't really argue about that. But I will say, I don't know whether or not it was *logo*therapeutic, but it *was* part of the therapeutic process…So my guess is that you're gonna be able to say, yes, my experience has been logotherapeutic, and I think grad school was definitely a part of that, even if you weren't able to back that up at the time. My guess is when we get through with this [10-year follow-up interview] you're gonna be able to go back and say yes, this was logotherapeutic…It definitely was therapeutic. I just don't know that it was *logo*therapeutic.
Amber	Did it help your search for meaning in all of this?
Jesse	Absolutely!
Amber	Then that's logotherapy.
Jesse	It was part of the process. It's just I don't think I had found the meaning at that time.

I also asked Jesse to reflect on his career thus far, and tell me of what he was most proud. His response illustrates yet another way his talks are helping to heal some very deep and very old wounds—his own, but society's as well:

> I spoke at a university in the early spring…And after the presentation they had a dinner for me, where only you know, like 20 people, 20 students or whatever were invited. They wined and dined me. It still blows me away that sometimes I'm a big deal, but they were treating me like I was this really big deal…so then we went to this other room and…there was food there. I ended up sitting next to the director of diversity… And she was an African American woman, so she was a person with her own experiences, I'm sure…And toward the end of dinner—And we weren't talking as a group. We were just chatting. The student next to her said, "I'm really surprised you're here. Don't you have church on Wednesday night?" And

> she said, "Yeah. I was only going to stay for the first 20 min, but the Holy Spirit was present, and I knew I had to stay. The Holy Spirit was present at this talk." ...Now those aren't my beliefs, so it's not like I was moved because of that. But I respect her way of looking at the world, and that was *huge* to me. And that kind of reminded me that I'm doing good work... Especially with the history of Christianity and people like me.

Jesse Inside the "Well-Lit, Warm Room," Ten Years Later

More than a decade after Jesse first responded to Frankl's quote about the "well-lit, warm and pleasant lecture room," I asked him to read it again and tell me his thoughts. Years ago, Jesse talked about how the metaphor matched his actuality of speaking in well-lit rooms across campus. He then narrowed his response to the same excerpt that had also caught Gillian's attention: "Emotion, which is suffering, ceases to be suffering as soon as we form a clear and precise picture of it" (Frankl 1946/2014, p. 69). He resonated with Frankl's assertion that these talks can "objectify" personally sensitive issues. His research, too, was a platform from which he could articulate his own "clear and precise picture" of gender.

Post-tenure and in his second academic position, Jesse naturally focused on different things when I asked him about the quote. First, he was particularly hesitant to compare his experience as a transgender man with someone imprisoned in a death camp. But he also understood from Frankl's other writings that the comparison is not necessary:

> There's part of me that says, "Oh I can't possibly compare my experience to someone in a camp, because that's about as close to hell on earth as you can get." But as you know I love the Frankl perspective that suffering is a gas. It fills you up, so don't ever compare your suffering to someone else and negate it.

Again, Jesse noticed the final part of Frankl's quote:

> And then he said, "Emotion, which is suffering, ceases to be suffering as soon as we form a clear and precise picture of it."...You know where he says, "I became disgusted with the state of affairs which compelled me, daily and hourly, to think of only such trivial things" meaning all of the misery, so "I forced my thoughts to turn to another subject", and he visualizes himself in the well-lit room? So he stopped thinking about what he

> *didn't* want, and started thinking about what he *did* want. That's a real technique for…for growth. And one that I've followed for several years. [I say to myself] the moment may suck, but what would I *like* for the moment? I don't like where I am. Where would I like to be? And don't spend so much time thinking about what's wrong. Think about what's right. And there's real value in that. But the danger—that's little bit strong—but the danger in that is further burying feelings.
> I was sitting right here one night, and I was having a lot of back pain. Not pain. I was uncomfortable. I was uncomfortable in my body. And I was trying to focus on the positive and all of that. And finally I just said, you know, [long pause] "Dammit, there's been some things in my life that have been hard. You know, there have just been some hard—*I have been through some stuff.*" And I quit trying to focus on the positive, and just put my attention on what was, and what is. And in that moment I was not feeling good in my body…And there was something about *acknowledging* that…And I'm choosing this word very consciously, that was very sacred. There was something *sacred* about acknowledging the pain of the past and of the present… I just went, "You know, I'm really feeling sad about this thing that happened to me 20 years ago, and I'm just gonna sit here and feel sad." And it lifted within a few minutes. And then when I read, "Emotion, which is suffering, ceases to be suffering as soon as we form a clear and precise picture of it". And what I was saying was "emotion, which is suffering, ceases to be suffering as soon as we quit fighting it and allow it to be what it is, and accept it as part of our history and part of who we are." It's just another level of self-acceptance.

I then asked Jesse if he still saw himself on that metaphorical platform in the well-lit, warm room. He replied:

> Absolutely. Yeah. I sometimes feel that I am at my absolute best when I am in front of a group of people talking. That's when I'm in the zone…When I'm in front of people—He visualizes it as a well-lit room. I visualize it as a stage. When I'm on stage, that's where I'm at my best.

Conclusions

When Jesse started graduate school, he had two meaningful goals. First, he wanted to gain self-understanding through engaging in academic work. Second, he wanted to do research that would call into question the dichotomous two-sex/gender paradigm. Although he was not able to attack the dichotomous paradigm directly in his dissertation, he did use his argument as a theoretical foundation in other work. The developmental insights Jesse inserted seamlessly into his narrative during his interviews demonstrated that graduate school did contribute to his goal of self-understanding. He was also able to find meaning through his gender presentations—an opportunity that he had not foreseen when he applied for the Ph.D. program. These talks were meaningful because of their value as part his coming-out process, and for their role in educating others. Education might help other atypically gendered people have an easier time out in the world. Ultimately they became a source of joy for him. It is also worth reiterating that in Jesse's statement of purpose, he was not willing to risk using the word "transgender." By the time he completed his dissertation, he was approaching a place of being totally comfortable with his identity as an atypically gendered person, and was confident enough to deal with people who weren't comfortable with that identity. So much so, that by the time he graduated, he had fully embraced his humanity: The following quote beautifully expresses this significant consequence of Jesse's search for meaning in graduate school:

> I will never say "I'm a person who's transgender." *I am a transgender person*......that is *such* a big part of my identity. And I embrace that...to such an extent now, that I will never downplay...how much...that defines who I am by saying "I'm a person who's transgender." I am a transgender person...That is *very* okay...That's who I am.

As Jesse's friend, I will attest that he is also much more than this. But his point is well-taken. When we are together doing things that are not related to the present research project, his gender identity is not something I think about much. But I also realize that in saying this, I am coming from a place of straight privilege. I don't *have* to think about it. Jesse does, in no small part because many of the people he encounters daily on the street or in the halls of the academy *are* thinking about his gender. I find it heroic the way he has embraced this burden of constantly having to explain his nature to others, and his gracious, gentle approach with people who don't yet understand. He even sees humor in it. In clarifying for me one of the advantages of being good at teaching a notoriously difficult subject, he said, "If you can teach statistics to non-researchers and non-statisticians, you can get away with *a lot*, including being transgender!" ...[It's as if the students are saying], "Okay fine. If you can teach statistics I'll call you 'he!'"

Nearing the end of our interview, I asked Jesse how his scholarship—inclusive of graduate school and his nearly ten years as a professor—has impacted his personal life. His answer supports his earlier assertion that the academy has served some logotherapeutic purposes:

> I'm *so* much happier that I used to be...And I think the talks and all of that has been part of the process of getting where I am...I had forgotten how to be happy. I had been unhappy for *so* long. I was three years old when this whole thing started. I'd forgotten how to be happy. And a few years ago I thought, "Hmm. I've learned how to do a lot of things. I think I can learn how to be happy. I just need to figure out what that's gonna take and do it. And I have...So all of that stuff, all of the talks and all that had been part of the process. And so the biggest impact is I have, and continue to move into, a place of happiness and contentment.

My interview with Jesse ends just in time for me to leave for the airport. After taking a few goofy pictures with Jesse and his wife, I pack my car and am off. Driving away I am able to see Jesse and Liz disappear into their house. Happiness and contentment? Check.

Jesse's Advice for Scholar Activists

- Be very good at what you do. If you're good at what you do, especially if you're doing something that's valued, people will accept a lot. And it's harder to be denied tenure if you're very good at what you do.
- If you want to be researcher, take as many inquiry courses as you possibly can. And make sure you understand the material, because you do not want your methodology coming under fire. There are people who will want to tear down your work because they don't agree with it. Don't give them fuel for criticizing your methodology. Make sure that it is sound.
- People who don't like your message will sometimes attack the messenger. If you want to practice your scholarship in a public way, you might to think about this before you take your shirt off and flash your breasts at *Mardi Gras*. That stuff can come back and haunt you.

- Sometimes activist scholars are motivated by anger. This makes sense. There is a lot of injustice in the world. However, if anger is a problem for you, work on that. If you try to out-anger someone, all you do is end up with more anger. Do you want to live in an angry world?
- Do your own internal work, whether it's spiritually or through therapy. If you don't want your issues to come into play in your scholarship, then work on your issues. Being an academic, and doing the activist work you want to do, can be part of the process, but it is not a good idea for this to be the only way to work on your issues.

References

American Psychological Association. (2015). Guidelines for psychological practice with transgender and gender nonconforming people. *American Psychologist, 70*(9), 832–864.

Ellis, C. (2004). *The ethnographic I: A methodological novel about autoethnography*. Walnut Creek, CA: AltaMira.

Ellis, C. (2007). Telling secrets, revealing lives: Relational ethics in research with intimate others. *Qualitative Inquiry, 13*(1), 3–29.

Fine, M. (1994). Working the hyphens: Reinventing the self and other in qualitative research. In N. Denzin & Y. Lincoln (Eds.), *Handbook of qualitative research* (pp. 70–82). Thousand Oaks, CA: Sage.

Frankl, V. E. (1946/2014). *Man's search for meaning*. Boston: Beacon Press.

Intersex Society of North America. (2008). *MYTH #10: Intersex is extremely rare*. Retrieved from http://www.isna.org/faq/ten_myths/rare.

Kübler-Ross, E. (1969). *On death and dying*. New York: Routledge.

Owton, H., & Allen-Collinson, J. (2013). Close but not too close: Friendship as method(ology) in ethnographic research encounters. *Journal of Contemporary Ethnography, 43*(3), 283–305.

Tillmann-Healy, L. (2001). *Between gay and straight: Understanding friendship across sexual orientation*. New York: Rowman & Littlefield.

Tillmann-Healy, L. (2003). Friendship as method. *Qualitative Inquiry, 9*(5), 729–749.

CHAPTER 4

Theoretical Physics: Building a Time Machine to Save My Father

This trying to attain the unattainable…That bittersweet part. I suspected it was going to be there the older I got, and the more I learned about physics. But I knew that was something I still had to go for, because…that's the thing that gave meaning to me in my personal life, was the love that I had for my father, the love I still have for my father…The universe has given me things, and I've given things back. It's given me meaning, [like] the Schrödinger[1] Equation, you know, and I've given back, with teaching. And that's been satisfying. It's been a satisfying life… And I feel blessed that I've been able to do that. I mean how many people get the opportunity to be paid to study about the universe itself? I mean it's about as close to theology as you can get without being a theologian.

—Ronald Mallett, Theoretical Physicist, 2017

I meet Ronald Mallett for the first time at a cozy Italian restaurant near the University of Connecticut. The cheery reception from the waitstaff clues me in that he is a regular there. He knows their names, and he introduces me as a young researcher who has come from "all the way from Texas" to interview him. He seems tickled by this fact, even though he's been interviewed by dozens of reporters and writers over the years, and he is the focus of two feature-length documentaries (*How to Build a Time Machine*, 2016; *The World's First Time Machine*, 2003). Next

[1] Edwin Schrödinger (1887–1961) was an Austrian physicist. The Schrödinger equation is fundamental to the study of quantum mechanics.

A. Esping, *Epistemology, Ethics, and Meaning in Unusually Personal Scholarship*, https://doi.org/10.1007/978-3-319-73718-8_4

week he will be traveling to Austria for a screening of the most recent one. I can tell our server is curious about this new development, and I'm quite sure she didn't know that this kind and jovial customer is actually a famous theoretical physicist. I hope she googles his name when she gets off work. His autobiography, *Time Traveler: A Scientist's Personal Mission to Make Time Travel a Reality* (Mallett and Henderson 2007), will blow her mind.

Ron is a tall African American man, and he looks and moves much younger than his 73 years. Today he is wearing a dark suit and a tie bedecked with Einstein's famous $E = mc^2$ equation in a variety of particolored fonts. When I comment that I like his tie, he beams. "I wore this just for you," he says. After lunch, we tour the University of Connecticut and visit the laboratory space he shares with another physicist. Apparently this laboratory used to be a mental hospital, and Ron delights in telling me this. He shows me the ring laser he built and does his best to penetrate my ignorance and explain the significance of this device to—eventually—time travel. He lights up when he is teaching. Unlike many elite professors, he enjoyed shepherding undergraduates through introductory courses, and his patience with me is testament to this affinity. By the end of the lesson, I actually think I understand the concepts, if not the equations.

The tour ends at his home, where we sit for the formal interview. Behind me is a cabinet of physics curiosities. There is a small model of the time machine depicted in the 1960 film version of H. G. Wells' novel, *The Time Machine* (Wells 1895/2017), a DeLorean, an hourglass, and some commercially produced religious-style candles depicting the "Patron Saints of Time Travel."[2] I recognize three names: Albert Einstein, Stephen Hawking, and Ronald Mallett.

Ron's story is a love story about a boy and his father. And it is, at times, a sad story. It has many essentials of a bankable Hollywood script, including tragedy, resilience, and an unlikely hero to triumphs against the odds. But it would be a mistake to get lost in the poetry and forget that this lovely man is also hard-core intellectual, a nose-to-the-grindstone scholar, and a tenured full professor who was the first person to solve Einstein's gravitational field equations for a ring laser and a circulating cylinder of light (Mallett 2003). And he did all of this as an African

[2]These are produced by artist Mickey Duzyj and writer Jon Korn and marketed by Echo Park Time Travel Mart in Los Angeles, CA.

American who grew up in the era of Jim Crow. When he earned his Ph.D. in 1973, he was one of only 79 African American physicists in the USA, working in a discipline that boasted around 20,000 members at the time. When he was hired by the University of Connecticut in 1975, he was their first African American physicist. There were no African Americans working alongside him in Chemistry, Biology, or Engineering. Nearly 50 years later, he says, he still belongs to a "rare species."

Ron was born in 1945 in the Bronx, New York, the son of Boyd Mallett, a television repair technician, and his wife, Dorothy. An "electronics whiz" known for his unusual skill in his job, Boyd Mallett helped to wire the brand-new United Nations building in Manhattan. Ron smiles when he lists some of the celebrities, like Walter Matthau and Jackie Cooper, for whom he also rendered service. "I idolized him," Ron recounts. I always thought of my father as sort of "the television repairman to the stars." Calling his father the "center of his life," and recalling that his childhood days "began and ended with him," he lists some of the qualities that drew people to his dad. He was "a character" with a delightful sense of humor and a penchant for good-natured teasing. He sometimes worked two jobs, but family was always the most important thing. He helped stimulate Ron's intellectual curiosity by bringing home scientific toys like gyroscopes and crystal radio sets, and then spent time helping Ron and his siblings figure out how they worked. Boyd also made Ron earn his 25-cent allowance by answering multiplication problems. Ron wasn't always thrilled with this task, but he "understood that he was trying to get the importance of education across to me." As Ron grew older, his dad began to teach him about the inner workings of television sets. Perhaps someday the Malletts would start a TV repair business together:

> I was the oldest of the four children, and I think I thought of myself as sort of the heir apparent because he was beginning…to show me things behind the television set…I knew he wanted to go out to Long Island to have his…own store, eventually. And I think he wanted me to go into business…with him, which is something I would have loved to have done.

Although he looked robust and healthy, Ron's father died unexpectedly from a heart attack when he was only 33 years old, and Ron was only ten. It was a devastating loss for the little boy. Ron was inconsolable and plunged into a deep and long depression. Ron described this abject despair in his autobiography:

> I was aware that something had happened inside of me. It was as if I had shut down, and was just going through the motions. Once a naturally exuberant child with a gregarious personality I became withdrawn and sullen. My father's absence left a void in my life that nothing seemed to fill. The how-and-why questions I had always put to him now went unasked. Schoolwork lost its meaning, as I knew there would be no more weekly quizzes that I needed to be sharp for…It was unbearable to think I would never be able to meet him at the end of the day at his subway stop. I was always so overjoyed to be in his presence, and thrilled when he let me carry his toolbox the rest of the way home. With his sudden and unexpected departure from my life, my childhood ended, and happiness was no longer my natural state. In a real way, part of me was lost forever. (Mallett and Henderson 2007, p. 10)

When I met Ron to interview him for the present book, he elaborated:

> To say it brought my world crashing down really doesn't get at the depth of it. I mean *I really didn't care* anymore weather I lived or died…If he had said, after he was dead, "Do you want to come with me?" I would *gladly* have given up my life to have gone with him.

Books That Changed Ronald Mallett's Life

One of the intellectual gifts Ron inherited from his father was a precocious love of reading. After his father's death, Ron withdrew into a world of magazines, books, and movies, finding particular solace and a sense of escape in the fantasy and science fiction genres:

> I really was a book-aholic. I mean a *serious* book-aholic. My mother would give us whatever she could as far as getting lunches at school. And I would go to the Salvation Army, which you could go to and get paperback books for five cents. And I would spend it on that. And I was getting thinner and thinner and thinner. In fact eventually I got secondary anemia, and she took me to the doctor and …they realized I wasn't eating properly. [*laughing*] And so that stopped. So I started going to junk yards and selling rags and things like that in order to feed my book habit.

When Ron was eleven, he came across a 1956 *Classics Illustrated* comic book version of the H. G. Wells' novel, *The Time Machine* (Wells 1895/2017). The protagonist is an inventor and scientist who builds a device that takes him far into Earth's future, and back again. More than 60 years later, Ron can still quote the opening line from memory:

> And right at the beginning of it, at the very very opening line, it said, "Scientific people know very well that time is just a kind of space. We can move forward and backward in time just as we can move forward and backward in space."

This was a revelation, and the beginning of an obsession that would motivate Ron for the next six decades—through adolescence, a stint in the Air Force, college, graduate school, and ultimately, through promotion and tenure as a theoretical physicist: He was going to build a time machine so he could go back to 1955 and save his father:

> When I read that I thought, "Wait a minute. You mean it might be possible to actually move forward and backward in time? And if it's possible to move *backward* in time, then maybe I could build a time machine and go back and see [my father] again." I took that very seriously as an 11 year-old.

The cover of the comic contained an illustration of what Wells' time machine might look like. Using this as a model, Ron went down into the basement where his mother had stored ephemera, including his father's leftover television and radio parts, and he built his first time machine:

> I tried using bicycle parts and all kinds of radio parts to try to put something together. And of course nothing happened. And I was disappointed, but not discouraged because I remembered [the comic book] said "*scientific* people know very well." I wasn't sure exactly what that meant but I knew that it meant that I had to have more understanding.

At eleven, Ron didn't know what that "more understanding" entailed, so he just kept reading—mostly science fiction, since at this age, he didn't really understand the difference between science fiction and actual science. He sought out Wells' original novel, *The Time Machine* (1895/2017), which he described as "a little bit more rough going" for a young boy. (He used a dictionary to understand two of the words in the very first sentence of the book.) But this was the first step toward his scientific education.

Despite the all-consuming nature of his obsession with building a time machine, Ron did not tell anyone what he was doing. When I asked him to explain why he felt the need to keep it a secret, he reminded me that this was the 1950s, and time travel was not in the realm of legitimate science then: "You've got to remember that this was back before Sputnik, okay? People weren't even sure we could go into *space*, let alone this notion of time travel." Time travel was firmly quartered in the domain of science fiction, and science fiction was not at all the mainstream genre it is today. Smiling, Ron told me, "people thought if you were reading science fiction there was something not particularly right about you."

A couple of years later, Ron discovered the second book that would change his life. On a shelf of the local Salvation Army thrift store, he found *The Universe and Dr. Einstein* (Barnett 1948/2005). The cover showed Albert Einstein next to an hourglass:

> I knew that Einstein was this great genius. I didn't know what it was he did, but I knew he was this great genius…and here he was standing next to an hourglass which I knew represented time…I just put it together. I said, "Oh, maybe Einstein had something to do with time. So I got the paperback. And even though it was a popularization, it was rough rough going. But I got the essence of the book. It said that…unlike the old physics of Newton, where nothing can effect time, according to Einstein there *are* things you can do to alter time. You can actually *do* things that can *change* going through time. And that was it. That was the beginning for me…I thought, "Wait a minute. If I could understand what Einstein did then this might lead to the real possibility of a time machine. Because Einstein said that time can be altered." So that became the beginning of my passion for Einstein…But I realized that was not going to be simple [*smiling*] because the physics behind trying to understand Einstein was *way* beyond anything that I could understand. So this was going to be a long journey.

Military and College

Ron knew that this journey to building a time machine would involve going to college. He would be the first in his family to do so. At first, he thought he would study electronic engineering, which he viewed as "a natural progression from what my father was." He entered the Air Force with the goal of eventually using the Vietnam Era GI Bill (VEGIB) to get this degree. He volunteered to work the undesirable graveyard shift monitoring a Strategic Air Command computer system because there would be ample downtime that he could use to read anything and everything he could get his hands on about science. Periodic trips to a nearby city for "book raids" kept him supplied with material. With the exception of one particularly kind and well-educated colleague, he did not discuss his love of science and science fiction. And he certainly didn't tell anyone about his goal of building a time machine. He connected the need for secrecy in the Air Force with the discretion he exercised even at age eleven:

> Even at that age, I *knew* that that was not going to be a good idea. Because they were already concerned about me. "And here's this kid wanting to build a time machine? He's got a serious problem here." So I kept it a secret. And this is the same thing that happened when I was in the Service. I couldn't tell them, you know, *why* I wanted to study these things. I mean I would have to keep it to myself...So I didn't let them know what it was that I was doing.

It was in the Air Force that Ron figured out that physics was his route, rather than engineering:

> It was during that time that I realized that it was going to have to be physics, rather than engineering, that I was going to have to study. Because Einstein was a physicist. And so that's when I switched to becoming a theoretical physicist. [*pause*] It goes a little deeper than that. It has to do with quantum mechanics, but that would be getting [*laughing*] way off into another tangent! But in any case, and that's what I did. I just had this singular focus.

After leaving the Air Force in 1966, Ron began taking courses toward a physics degree at the Altoona campus of Penn State. He no longer had to be an autodidact, but he was still learning all he could on the side about Einstein and time travel. And his ultimate goal was the same as it had been when he was eleven: Build a time machine, go back, warn his father.

> So you might say my interest in physics, and my interest in becoming a theoretical physicist, was due to this *passion* of wanting to see my father again. And it was a singular passion. I mean it was all-consuming. … But that focus was always there, even though other things were happening in my life. That had to happen. I mean for me that was the thing that was necessarily going to have to happen.

A painful breakup a year later led to Ron quitting college and moving to New York City with a new girlfriend. He found a job as a laboratory technician, using break times and lunches as opportunities to keep studying physics. One of his bosses, impressed by his diligence, convinced him to go back to school:

> And from that point on it didn't deviate. I just went more and more and more into physics. And I realized more and more as I was probing it, that Einstein's work *was* the path, that it *was* possible on a *scientific* basis, to not only travel to the future but to actually travel into the *past*. And I came to understand those aspects of his theory that would allow this.

Graduate School

In 1969, Ron finished his bachelors of science in Physics at Penn State's main campus, and one year later, he completed his master's degree. Due to his outstanding academic record, he was offered a National Science Foundation Traineeship, which helped to defray costs of his Ph.D. while also permitting him to spend extra time on research. He chose Gordon Fleming for his thesis advisor, in part because Fleming had a reputation for being a brilliant and kind professor, but also because he was working on something that Ron had already identified as important to understanding time travel. Working with Fleming would allow him to study something relevant to his secret goal, while also researching something that was solvable, new, and not likely to spark controversy:

> [Fleming] was looking at this thing called time reversal. But he wasn't looking at it in terms of a time machine… What he was doing is looking at how relativity looks at this time reversal process. He was looking at special relativity, which is Einstein's, you know, the effect of speed on time. What I knew, was that general relativity was going be the key to what *I* wanted in the long run. But what I decided, and I asked him, was I wanted to generalize *his* work into general relativity. That way I would learn more

about general relativity, and I would be doing something new with his work. And of course he agreed to that. If I had said, "Well I want to try to build a time machine." He would have said, "Ron, let's back up here."

Ron's thesis work with Dr. Fleming resulted in two publications in highly esteemed physics journals. He graduated with his Ph.D. In 1973, and after a short but important spell working with lasers in a private sector research laboratory, he accepted a tenure-track position at the University of Connecticut.

Becoming a Tenure-Track Professor

Ron did not disclose his unusually personal motivation for his research agenda at UConn either. He still viewed his goal of building a time machine as a noble "secret mission" that must be protected in order to manifest. He understood that it was of paramount importance to be taken seriously, and in the 1970s, time travel was still something that bordered in many people's minds on "crackpot science." Ron also knew that his status as a rare African American physicist—one of 79 in the country—also made him vulnerable:

> How many of those 79 do you think were at major universities? *Not very many of them.* And so I needed to be protected. I knew that I was an endangered species. And I knew that by saying what I was trying to do, I would become obsolete...Einstein's work was considered serious, but the *topic* in Einstein's work that I was interested in was considered fringe. [And] I was an African American physicist. Moreover, I was an African American *theoretical* physicist in Einstein's domain...Being a theoretical physicist specializing in Einstein's theory was considered to be *very*, very frontier. Very, very difficult. I knew that. And I wanted to be respected for that...It was going to be a *problem* if I was perceived as being beyond the fringe, beyond the pale. *And I did not want that*...I knew that I was at that time a very rare species. And you know what can happen to rare species if they are not careful.

Ron did not want to become extinct, so he "cloaked" his interest in building a time machine by focusing on related research topics:

> Fortunately for me, Einstein's work covered things like black holes, which became a specialty of mine. And black holes affect time. Which is good,

> because then I could study black holes, and study about how time was being affected, but keep that on the side. And so I've made my career on understanding Einstein's theories of Big Bang, black holes, and things like that. And that's how I was able to go through the tenure track. And it wasn't until...after I got tenure and became full professor [*laughing*], that I came out of the time travel closet.

While at UConn, Ron published more than two dozen papers on issues related to Einstein's theory of relativity, but he remained single-minded as to his ultimate purpose. These highly theoretical papers were a means to a very practical end:

> The *primary* focus is I need to have the space and time to concentrate on the physics that I need in order to figure out how build a time machine, in order to see my father again. [*taps table on each word of "I need to"*] *That* was the primary.

After receiving tenure and promotion to associate professor, Ron received a Ford Foundation Postdoctoral Fellowship and took a sabbatical year to study with John A. Wheeler. Wheeler had a distinguished pedigree. He was a former colleague of both Albert Einstein and J. Robert Oppenheimer, a student of famed quantum theorist Niels Bohr, and teacher to Richard Feynman. While working with Wheeler, he encountered the work of Stephen Hawking. By the end of his sabbatical, he had considerably advanced his work on black holes. The zeitgeist in theoretical physics was ripe for Ron's work. New understandings in the field were making time travel somewhat of a hot topic. Ron worked tirelessly on his problems, to the detriment of his physical health and some of his personal relationships, but in 2000 he published a landmark paper, "Weak Gravitational Field of the Electromagnetic Radiation in a Ring Laser." Although the article did not mention the words "time travel," it created a stir in the physics community. This was Ron's first applied step toward the ultimate goal of building his machine (Mallett and Henderson 2007).

Coming Out of the "Time Travel Closet"

Ron described finally being "dragged out of the time travel closet" in 2001 when a colleague asked him to talk about this work during a colloquium at the University of Michigan physics department:

> I'd made a breakthrough in the first part showing that circulating light can twist space. That was a necessary condition. In mathematics they have what's called necessary and sufficient conditions. In other words you have to have the necessary condition. The necessary condition was that circulating light twists space. That actually is something that can be relatively inexpensively demonstrated [at least in terms of theoretical physics experiments]...The next phase was to show that if you twist the space strongly enough you can twist time into a loop. That's two separate papers. So that was the sufficient condition. In any case, once I had the first part, there was a colleague of mine, a well-respected astrophysicist from the University of Michigan at Ann Arbor, [who] wanted me to give a colloquium about that. And I told him the work was incomplete. And he said, "That's okay. You can just say that." I wanted to give it a purely scientific title. I wanted to call it, "The Gravity of Circulating Light." And he said, "That's too dry." He said, "We're never going to get that many people to come."...And he said, "You're going to eventually lead this to time travel. Why don't we call it, 'The Gravity of Circulating Light: A Route to Time Travel.'"

Ron agreed. However, he didn't take into account that talks given in the well-regarded University of Michigan physics department were monitored by the press wire services. Two months before his scheduled talk, *New Scientist* magazine contacted him. After a few telephone conversations, the editor he had been speaking with requested a cover story. Even when he agreed to the article, Ron did not fully realize what this meant for the future of his career:

> One of my colleagues...When he heard that *New Scientist* was going to do a cover article on me, he said, "Ron, now you're going to become famous." I gotta tell you, the day before when I went on my email, I had maybe like half a dozen emails. The day after that article came out in *New Scientist*, I had page after page after page of emails from all over the world.

These emails were from both the lay public and from scientists, and many included invitations for interviews. Newspapers from *Pravda* in

Russia to *The Wall Street Journal* were interested in his time machine. This attention from the popular press was concerning, because this can sometimes make it harder for academics to be taken seriously among their peers. Ron wasn't sure his colleagues were reading those articles. He assumed that most of them were not. This is why he was nervous when he chose to finally reveal his backstory at a prestigious physics conference. Ultimately, this decision would become one of the proudest and most meaningful moments of Ron's academic—and personal—life.

In 2002, Ron was scheduled to give a talk to a worldwide group of relativity specialists gathered at the International Association for Relativistic Dynamics conference in Washington, DC. This would his first time revealing this work to a group of peers, and unlike this colloquium at the University of Michigan, this talk would involve "all the bells and whistles" and "the whole tensor calculus thing." There would be pages of calculations, and an audience equipped and eager to find any tiny flaw in the logic or mathematics. Given that he had also decided to finish the talk by sharing the unusually personal motivation for his work, Ron described being "almost *unnerved* by the fact of what I was going to be doing." He started with a joke about his hefty stack of transparencies, and then he began in earnest. He had spent the last few months working tirelessly to solve Einstein's gravitational field equation for a ring laser and a circulating cylinder of light. One morning at 3:00 am, he discovered in the equations closed loops in time which could, theoretically, lead to time travel to the past. Now he was sharing these equations with some of the world's most prominent theoretical physicists, demonstrating through his calculations "that space and time can be manipulated in a whole new way that would lead to the possibility of time travel into the past" (Mallett and Henderson 2007, p. 171). In a rare gesture for a professional physics conference, he ended his presentation with a photograph of his family. He told the story of his father's death and his reason for doing this work: "My original motivation for everything—learning math and science, going to college, becoming a physicist—was so I could see my father again" (Mallett and Henderson 2007, p. 171). And it was over.

A stunned silence followed. Then applause. Then insightful questions about the math and its implications. And finally, something extraordinary and beautiful happened. The legendary physicist Bryce DeWitt—a cofounder of the quantum theory of gravity—stood up and addressed

Dr. Mallett publically. "I don't know if you'll ever see your father again," he said, "but I do know he would have been proud of you."

Something healed in that moment. As much as the comment itself, the public nature of it mattered too. The significance was immediately apparent to Ron:

> Sometimes at these conferences people will talk to you afterwards, privately...What he did was *public*...And I can't tell you what that meant to me, to have a man of that stature say publicly—He could have said it privately. And he actually was *conscious* of what he was doing. Afterwards I thanked him... and he invited me to have lunch with him and his wife afterwards. But I can't tell you how much that meant to me that he did it publically. He could have taken me to the side and said, "You know, Mallett, I think that was a really good talk." But for him to actually say that to this audience!

In hearing Ron tell this story, I felt like I understood completely why that moment was so affirming and meaningful. What I wasn't sure of was why Ron chose to take the risk. He had been working in secret for nearly 50 years. Why reveal his goal now? Part of it can be attributed to his already earned respect from the field, his tenure, and his full professor rank. There was far less to lose professionally now. Another reason was that time travel was no longer a "crackpot" idea. It had been legitimized through the work of Einstein, Stephen Hawking, and others. And—bottom line—Ron *wanted* them to know.

> [Time travel] is actually a topic now that is done by serious physicists. Stephen Hawking, you know, and Kip Thorne, they talk about time travel now. But this generation grew up with *me*. We call ourselves the *Star Trek* generation. But the thing is that their interest is not personal. These people—I mean there's a whole group—but none of them have it from this personal angle. I have found that I am the only one who came at it not just because it was intellectually interesting, but came to it because it was a very *personal* motivation, that in fact, my entire life was based on. So I thought that this group would like to know that. Because they would think that my motivation was just like most of theirs, which is that this is an intellectually interesting topic, and I was looking at the scientific basis for it. But I wanted them to know that it was more than that, that it was not just simply an intellectually interesting topic, which it is, but that there was a very *personal* motivation that made me want to do this topic.

When I probed why that would be important for them to know this personal aspect of the work, he said,

> Why did I want them to know? I really can't tell you except for the fact that I felt that it was important for them to know that this was my motivation. That it wasn't just purely an intellectual exercise, but this was a personal theme that motivated me....Here it was equation after equation after equation after equation...But what was the motive behind this? And I thought it was interesting for them to know. Because I would like sometimes speakers to let me know....Obviously you're here doing this, but what was the background? What I was doing for them is what's important for me. I have read just about everything that's written about Einstein. But not just to know about his work, but to know *why*...You know, the *person*. I wanted to know the *person* behind it.

Painful Letters from the Public

Ron's work has captivated the general public. He gets letters nearly every day from people from around the world who are hopeful that he is close to completing his time machine. These letters are often from families who have lost a loved one, or from people who would like to go back and change devastating decisions. Some of these letters are heartbreaking. In our interview, he told me a harrowing story of one letter he received from a writer in Europe. He hadn't been able to read it at first because he wasn't fluent in the language. But he was able to guess the story from some enclosed photographs:

> The writer had sent me pictures with this letter...There were four pictures. One showed this middle aged couple with this twentysomething young woman in it. An ordinary looking couple. And then the second picture showed the woman in sort of a cute model-type pose, type of thing. The third picture showed this mangled vehicle. And the fourth picture showed her in a coffin...It brought tears to my eyes even now...So what I guessed was, just looking at the pictures until I had the translation of the letter, was that this middle aged couple were the father and mother of this woman. And that she had been in this crash and she had died. And when I got the translation what it was, was the father asking me if my work would lead to a time machine where he could send a message back to his daughter to prevent her from getting into that car and dying...That was one of the

> most poignant of them that I got, with the pictures and everything like that. But I get those almost on a daily basis.

Another writer enclosed a letter from her son, who was serving a life sentence for murder:

> Her son had seen a documentary that I had done some years ago called *The World's First Time Machine* (2003)...He was in prison for life for murdering his girlfriend. And he would want to go back and change that. He told me the details of the story. Well, he actually didn't murder *her*. He actually had mistaken her sister for her. So he actually murdered the wrong person, number one. But the fact that he murdered anyone...It was heartbreaking. Because clearly he's devastated. But the rest of his life he's going to be in there. This was a young man who was in his twenties. Can you imagine that?...So of course I responded, and said there wasn't anything that I could do.

Ron saves these letters, and when the writers are not "crackpots," he always responds. I asked him what he says to grieving people:

> I give them my heartfelt sympathy. And I tell them about the limitations of time travel, and that we're working on it. Because there's no way that I'm going to give these people a false hope about these things. But I tell them that it is, yes, possible, but there's still going to be these limitations...And they respond well. I mean they say, you know, "Thank you so much for responding."

I wondered, given the emotional salience of time travel for Ron and for the people who write to him on a daily basis, have any other theoretical physicists come forward who share his intensely personal reasons for studying time travel? Not yet. At this point, Ron believes he is still the only one.

Ronald L. Mallett Inside the "Well-Lit, Warm Room"

As with Gillian (Chapter 2) and Jesse (Chapter 3), I asked Ron to read Frank's quote about speaking at the podium in the "well-lit, warm and pleasant lecture room" (reproduced for readers in Chapter 1) and to tell me if the metaphor applied to his life and work. He compared Frankl's imagining himself after the war in a place of comfort and understanding to his own dream of being a physicist during those long, lonely night shifts spent reading about science in the Air Force:

> This thing about imagining…That is something that I would think that people do under stark circumstances that helps them to do things. Because one of the things that I enjoyed when I was in the Air Force is that sometimes the other technicians would ask me questions about the electronics and things like that. And they would call me "The Professor." That actually encouraged me, because I thought, you know, that would be a nice thing to be. You know, to have the respect of people like that. And that helped me to project how I could see myself in the future. And I think that this thing, at least for me, of projection, of…forgetting about what my circumstances are now, [and] thinking about what my life would be like *because* my circumstances are the way in which they are now. In other words, I'm going through all of this stuff right now—I was very lonely. But I actually *knew* that because I was doing all of this, I was eventually going to be in a place where I was going to get the things that I wanted *because* of the present.

I asked Ron if he had found that metaphorical "room" at UConn. He told me that he had, and that he realized, "Here I am. I actually have arrived. I actually *am* The Professor." But he also admitted that it is hard to slow down and bask in the fact that he is standing in Frankl's room:

> I actually think that I've got there in retrospect. The question is, do I feel like I'm there now? That is like trying to grasp on the present and hold it, especially when it's some pleasing things happening to you in the present. That's where I've always had the problem. The thing is enjoying the moment. And I think part of enjoying the moment is knowing that that moment is going to pass. So you might say that the well-lit place happens for me by reflecting on the past, and not the present. Because it flows. It's too ephemeral. It's past.

The media interest in Ron's story has opened doors for mentoring, which is something he appreciates doing from the comfort of that metaphorical "room." He is often asked to give talks to middle schools and high schools where he invites students to be passionate about their goals and then develop concrete strategies to get there. He is also part of an outreach program at UConn for underrepresented high school and university students who are interested in Science Technology Engineering

Mathematics (STEM) fields, particularly physics. Ron tells his own story of perseverance to these audiences because he hopes that the students will see that they, too, can find a way to pursue seemingly impossible dreams. But there is a downside. As we have already seen in the cases of the bereaved mother Gillian (Chapter 2) and the transgender researcher Jesse (Chapter 3), sharing one's story publically can be painful. Ron also acknowledged an emotional toll:

> It keeps reminding me constantly of the death of my father, which I think about anyway. But it reinforces that. And sometimes that can be—It can be [*sigh*]—I'm not sure of the word that I want to use. [*sigh*] It can be a bit taxing. Because it's hard sometimes to focus on what it means to be happy with my life as it *is*, because I keep thinking about my life as it *was*. You know I keep thinking about how happy I was when he was alive.

The darker thoughts usually happen when he is alone and away from the work he loves so much:

> The problem happens in the 4:00 in the morning, when I start thinking about my father. That's when things can sometimes go south a little bit. Because I'm not in the light of day anymore, and my father's still not with me. And so I still feel this wave of sadness that's associated with that, which I know that I'll feel until the day I die. And there's not really anything that I can do about that, except accept that, which I have. But it leeches a little bit of the joy that I *would* have. And I know that people would like me to be able to have more joy. Because it's like, "Don't you realize everything that you've accomplished?" Most people would feel thrilled. And yet you're just saying, "I'm satisfied", and it's not like, you know, "thrilled." And that's hard. And that's something that, to be honest, I'm still grappling with. But I know the source of it. It's not like this is a depression where you don't know where it's coming from. I actually know the source of it. It's just that, how do you deal with the source of it when you know what the source of it is? Because you can't banish it, because it's real, you know? I knew that I would miss [my father] every single day of my life, and I miss him every single day of my life. And I just haven't gotten over it. And of course…it becomes reinforced because people say "tell me the story." And as soon as I tell them the story, all of a sudden it brings it back to all that…So it's a fluid thing, this thing of standing myself in a warm, well-lit, pleasant lecture room. And I think that when Frankl's writing about this, he's writing about this because this is where he was now.

> The question is, is that even after all of his experiences, on a day to day basis, were there ever times in which [Frankl] felt that darkness coming in?

It is sometimes hard for Ron to prioritize happiness in the present when so much of his life has been focused on getting back to that happy time in the past. Perhaps Ron's well-lit, warm room resides in two temporal spaces: The future that he sees where time travel is possible, and the past where he finds memories of a much beloved father. This has made it more difficult for him, because "being happy" is a condition of the present:

> It makes it hard for me to focus on what it means to be happy as opposed to what it means to be successful. In other words, I'm successful in having achieved my goal. Even though I don't have the device, I have the theory behind the device. So that's going to be there even when I pass away…I have succeeded in knowing *how* it can be done. The problem is that I have been so goal-oriented for decades, that I don't know how to get off the train. That's a problem. That really is a problem…I only have one lever. And it's always forward. I don't know how to step off. And I don't even know exactly what that means. For example, even in the research that I'm continuing—I'm continuing this research because—I don't know how to—If I stop–I *dream* about physics! You know, I mean just last night I dreamt that I was in a classroom, you know. I have a hard time trying to figure out [*pause*] what it means to be happy as opposed to what it means to be successful. My life has meaning because of my goal.

When I suggest to Ron that he does not want to rest on his laurels, he tells me of a new meaningful goal that is oriented toward both his future and the past. He would like to see his life story on the big screen. There's been prior interest (Spike Lee once bought the rights), and there is renewed attention from other quarters. Ron's reason for wanting to see the movie echoes his reason for wanting to build his device in the first place. The movie, like the time machine, will allow him to see his father again:

Ron What I want to see is a feature film with a representation of my father on the big screen. That's what I want to see. I want to see an actor who's portraying him even more than I want to see an actor who's portraying me. I want to see that representation. I want to *live* through that…I will be able to project...In order to really enjoy a movie, that's what you do. You suspend things, and you allow yourself to become part of that movie for that little while. And so if they make a feature film of me and my relationship with my father, then I will be able to suspend my imagination and become a part of that movie and *live* through that representation they have of me as this little boy, of this man that they have as my father...

Amber It strikes me rather poetically as that is almost like an opportunity to see your dad again.

Ron I couldn't have said it better. I couldn't have stated it more accurately. So that's why this [movie] has become now a *huge* focus and mission for me.

Ronald L. Mallett's Legacy

Ron's Ph.D. students are currently serving in faculty positions throughout the country. This is one important legacy he is leaving for the academy, and perhaps also for the promise of time travel. However, it turns out that the feature film will be the only way for Ron to see his father again during his lifetime. There are two reasons. First, at 73 he understands he does not have enough of his own time left to complete the work he started. He will leave that inheritance for others. (The proceeds from a successful feature film may help to advance this aim by providing research funding.) But there is another reason. Ron's solution to Einstein's gravitational field equations with the ring laser and the circulating light cylinder demonstrated that the closed loops in time are produced by the circulating light. This is the on-off switch. When built, the machine could only travel back in time to the point when the device was first turned on. Since this will of course occur after Boyd Mallett died, there will be no way back to him. Ron still has few regrets.

> This trying to attain the unattainable...That bittersweet part. I suspected it was going to be there the older I got, and the more I learned about physics. But I knew that was something I still had to go for, because... that's the thing that gave meaning to me in my personal life, was the love that I had for my father, the love I still have for my father...The universe has given me things, and I've given things back. It's given me meaning, [like] the Schrödinger Equation, you know, and I've given back, with teaching. And that's been satisfying. It's been a satisfying life... And I feel

> blessed that I've been able to do that. I mean how many people get the opportunity to be paid to study about the universe itself? I mean it's about as close to theology as you can get without being a theologian.

Conclusions

Near the end of our interview, Ron shared a quote from one of Stephen King's *Dark Towers* books. When people try to do honorable things, he says, "They have not forgotten the face of their fathers." So I asked Ron to tell me how his work in academia has honored the face of his father. Here is his response:

> My work broadens our human understanding about the way in which the universe works. My father was always curious about how things work. I mean, that was his thing. How things work. And for me to do it on that *scale*—Plus being a teacher. I mean I've taught literally thousands of students. And I know that I have affected the lives of many of them, because many of them have told me…And all these things are for good of people, for the good of humanity. To me that honors him. When you do something good in the community it puts honor to the name of your family. To me that's the best thing you can do is to bring honor to your family. Not only honor to your family, but honor to people…My notion of what is me is more than just being an African American. I'm part of a historic lineage that goes all the way back to Galileo and Archimedes, and to do honor to my science by moving it forward in a positive way. These are all good things. I know that I've brought honor to his name.

Sitting across from Ron Mallett in his living room, I can attest that he is a deeply honorable man. He maintains that the death of his father is "what has made me the person that you see." So we wonder together, what life might have been for him had his father lived. It's a question he has often pondered.

> Once again it's what Bryce DeWitt said, "I don't know if you'll see your father again, but he would have been proud of you."…Would I change anything that has led to this? No. But the question that one could ask is, [what] would I have become if my father *hadn't* died? That's a whole different thing…in fact, this writer, she did a beautiful job of it… saying that in another parallel world there's a sign that says, "Mallett and Son

Television Repair." And I believe that that's what would have happened in that alternate world.

And with this poignant and beautiful image, we conclude our interview. Ron shows me a treasured photo album containing pictures of important physics colleagues, dear friends, and his family. He looks like his daddy. Maybe Ron has found a way after all, to bring his father back from the past. He's fixing ring lasers now, not televisions.

Ronald L. Mallett's Advice for Graduate Students Considering Unusually Personal Scholarship

- It's okay to strive for a seemingly unattainable goal. Human beings are at their best when they are working on difficult technological challenges.
- Many faculty members want to work with students who will extend what they are already doing. You may not be able to work on your own idea right away. Find a faculty member who is doing something related to what you are interested in—perhaps a small step along the way of your ultimate goal. Learn as much as you can about this related topic.
- Remember that you don't have to do everything now. You can continue to develop your idea *after* you have received your degree. Or tenure. Or full professor.
- When picking a thesis or dissertation topic, choose a problem to work on that is both solvable and new.
- Physics is a *calling*. Expect to spend thousands of silent hours grueling over laboratory apparatus and breaking your head against equations. It's great if you want to build a time machine. Just don't forget about the decades of math and physics that have to happen first. This is how you earn the respect of others in this priesthood.
- If at the end of your life you really wished you had done something, you should have done it. Find a way. Even the kids at Hogwarts do homework.

Ronald L. Mallett's Advice for Faculty Advisors

- Don't be a hoarder. Help students find their passion, even if it isn't in your lab. Invite brand-new students to visit with other faculty. They may need more information to make sound decisions. You'll both be glad if you take this step.
- Your students' personal well-being is extremely important. They are not machines. Their personal lives will impact their work. Don't pry, but to the extent that it is welcomed show interest in your students' personal lives.

References

Barnett, L. (1948/2005). *The universe and Dr. Einstein*. Mineola, NY: Dover.

Mallett, R. L. (2003). The gravitational field of a circulating light beam. *Foundations of Physics, 33*, 1307.

Mallett, R. L., & Henderson, B. (2007). *Time traveler: A scientist's personal mission to make time travel a reality*. New York: Basic Books.

Wells, H. G. (1895/2017). *The time machine*. Seattle, WA: Amazon Classics.

CHAPTER 5

Bioethics: Helping My Husband Die

Since I'd always worked in bioethics I knew quite a lot about medicine generally… because I'd been around that all this time. And then to be the patient and the patient's principal family member is—and every doctor who's ever been sick says the same thing, "I never really understood it until I was the patient." So suddenly you're on the receiving end of this. You recognize it intellectually, but it feels different… has a much greater reality, because it's not just about somebody else out there who's broken their neck. It's about you.

—Margaret Pabst Battin, Bioethicist, 2017

When I meet Peggy for the first time at her home, she welcomes me warmly, and with gracious hospitality. She has already made coffee for us. I believe the coffee serves two purposes. Peggy is thoughtful and kind, but she is also focused and ready to get to work. At 76 years old, she is every bit the formidable scholar her impressive vita lead me to expect, but far more approachable. She speaks slowly, in measured tones, as if every word counts, and since later I will be personally transcribing hours and hours of interviews, it does. Stacks of books, papers, and journals ornament many of the surfaces in her home. Recalling my own house, which is more likely to be cluttered with dog toys and laundry, I think, "Now *this* is what a professor's house should look like." She offers the coffee, and we chat outside, getting to know one another. Her cat joins us, and I admire the ancient, serpentine wisteria winding its way around her house.

A. Esping, *Epistemology, Ethics, and Meaning in Unusually Personal Scholarship*, https://doi.org/10.1007/978-3-319-73718-8_5

Considered one of the "mothers of bioethics," Peggy Battin is the author, co-author, or editor of more than 20 books, and first or sole author on more than one hundred journal articles. As a philosopher, her interests are as varied as they are deep, and she has published on such topics as religion, aesthetics, birth control, and infectious disease. However, she is best known for her expertise in end-of-life decision making. Relevant book titles include *The Least Worst Death: Essays in Bioethics on the End of Life* (Battin 1994), *Physician-Assisted Suicide: Expanding the Debate* (Battin et al. 1998), *The Case for Physician-Assisted Dying: The Right to Excellent End-of-Life Care and Patient Choice* (Quill and Battin 2004), and *Ending Life: Ethics and the Way We Die* (Battin 2005). A prominent champion of voluntary euthanasia and physician aid in dying, she is a first call for legal teams and legislators looking for guidance. During the two days I spent at her home, her phone was constantly signaling that new messages had come in. From our conversations I know that at that time she was fielding calls and emails from, among other important people, a US Senator's office and a legal team in the UK, both seeking input. It seemed a typical week for Peggy.

Beyond her professional accomplishments, aspects of Peggy's personal story are extraordinary. Her academic career is bookended by two formative experiences with death—one chosen, one not. Her mother, Margaret Richards Pabst, died naturally in 1962 after a lengthy decline from liver cancer. Peggy was in her junior year of college. More than 50 years later Peggy's husband, a much beloved English literature professor named Brooke Hopkins, was gravely injured in a bicycle accident that left him a very high quadriplegic, ravaged by constant infections and completely dependent on machines and other people for every vital function. Approximately five years later, he chose to have his life brought to an end. The intervening years tell Peggy's story of a uniquely personal connection to scholarship.

Peggy's early life was unusual for a woman born in the USA in 1940. For one thing, both of her parents held Ph.Ds. Her mother earned a doctorate in mathematical economics from Columbia in 1944—a time when few women so dared. Her father was an expert in statistical quality control whose work brought the family to India for a time during Peggy's adolescence. Peggy inherited their ambition and sense of adventure, choosing to study philosophy and spend a year studying in

Munich during her junior year in college. It was during this trip abroad she received news that her mother was dying. Peggy was aware that her mother had been treated for cancer, but her parents, wanting her to enjoy the opportunity in Munich, kept her from knowing when it recurred. In the slower times before Skype and email, this was easier to do. Moreover, physicians in the 1960s generally avoided words like "dying" even when this was an imminent fact. Indeed, the vast majority of physicians at that time opted to keep patients hopeful even in light of an irrefutably terminal diagnosis. In the spring of her junior year abroad, Peggy received a letter with the news, "This is the end, and if you can, come home." She did, and her mother died about two weeks later.

This experience had a profound impact on Peggy, both because of her compressed experience of what was in actuality, a lingering death, but also because of one of the last things she heard her mother say. In some ways, things had been going very well. Her mother was receiving what was for the 1960s the very best medical and palliative care, and she was dying at home among loved ones. But Peggy remembers a day when her mother left her bed to try to make it to the bathroom, which was not very far away. En route she collapsed at the foot of some stairs. Peggy heard her ask, "Why should it be so hard to die?" She would later describe watching her mother die as "*the* formative experience in my intellectual life" and something foundational to both her intellectual and emotional engagement with the world. She did not realize it at the time, but she was about to become a pioneer in a brand-new field—the study of ethical issues in biological and medical research and treatment. We now call this field "bioethics."

Peggy's early efforts at working through her loss foreshadowed what the field of bioethics would eventually become. After finishing her undergraduate degree in philosophy, she was admitted to Yale on a philosophy fellowship. As would be expected of many women of her era, she chose to marry instead of accepting this honor. Her first husband's job took them to California, and she channeled her intellectual energy into fiction writing, eventually taking some community writing courses in the evening while raising two young children. Her fiction was haunted by her mother's question, "Why should it be so hard to die?" It often focused on medical issues and questions of autonomy and truth-telling, that would later become "the stuff of bioethics":

> The stories that I wrote...were often about these topics, end of life, bioethics, and the way these things change, the way people interact, and stuff like that...And so I continued to write stories more or less like this, or drawing on the same range of issues, because there still was no field of bioethics. Or at least not one that I knew anything about. There were a couple of people writing, but there were no courses...but a realm of experience for which the fiction writing was basically the only outlet. Or the only way of—It's not an outlet so much. A way of [*pause*]—I'm looking for the right word and not finding it. I'm thinking about processing or digesting, but none of those are quite the right terms. It's a matter of deeper engagement. The death and dying stuff had become somehow really interesting.

I probed. By "interesting" did Peggy mean therapeutic? Certainly Gillian (Chapter 2) and Jesse (Chapter 3) found academic work to be therapeutic. And academia gave Ron Mallett a sense of purpose that could be characterized that way (Chapter 4). Peggy, however, would not endorse this interpretation, finding the word "therapeutic" to be "too superficial" for describing the role of fiction writing in her grief:

> "Therapeutic" suggests that you've got some kind of problem or illness that you want to cure. And I think this was not that. Of course the death was painful. I think I thought this way because of the Existentialist stuff. You don't want to cure grief. That's an important part of your experience as a human being, to be aware of death. So therapy would get rid of it. And you don't want that. Or you shouldn't want that. That's the easy, as they say, *inauthentic* way of dealing with this stuff.

I tried again; "So did the fiction writing help you understand what you were thinking and feeling? Is that a way to characterize it?"

> No. I think I'd put it a different way. It's not that you have something going on that you write fiction to try to cope with. It's that you have something going on that provides the material for creating these stories. Not that you write only about that, but—it provides the—it sounds a little trite to say creative energy or creative impulse or creative fodder or something like that. But because of the closeness of this experience, of seeing how people interact...Well the only word that keeps coming back is "engagement." Just something that is there that you turn into fiction that is of course addressed to an audience...Because remember [at that time] there's not too much discussion of these things.

One evening at a cocktail party for her children's school Peggy had a fortuitous introduction to a University of California Irvine (UCI) philosophy professor. Impressed that she had turned down a fellowship from Yale, he encouraged her to apply to UCI. She was admitted to the Ph.D. program in philosophy shortly thereafter. Eager to continue developing as a writer, she enrolled in the UCI fiction writing MFA concurrently with the Ph.D. She completed both degrees full time while also raising two young children.

Graduate School and Becoming Faculty

Peggy's undergraduate philosophy degree was typically generalist in nature, but it did introduce themes that helped shape her thinking about death and dying:

> In a philosophy program you read a lot of Existentialist stuff because that's what really engages undergraduates. But also Heidegger…is very attentive to issues about death and dying. So the Existentialist message is, let the imminence of death operate in your everyday life. Keep in mind the fact that you could die at practically any moment. Don't keep death away. Let it operate in your consciousness. So that's one thing that reinforced still thinking about the death of the mother. Well the death of the mother of course didn't occur until my junior year in college, and I'd read much of this stuff before that. But that made it all right to even think about it. Because remember this is before anybody would talk about it in a clinical setting.

Peggy's story echoes Gillian's here, albeit in a far more intellectualized way. For Gillian, reading research about other bereaved parents helped normalize her experience of grief in the aftermath of her son's death. This work also gave her language to conceptualize her experiences, and confidence to tell well-meaning (but ignorant) others that they were "wrong" in some of their advice. Just so, the Existentialist philosophy Peggy had been reading in college gave her permission to let the imminence of death operate in her consciousness—something that was already happening for her despite the admonitions of the early 1960s medical intelligentsia. Society would have had her push death away. She wanted to embrace its reality.

In graduate school, Peggy continued to cultivate bioethics themes in her fiction writing while also developing expertise in ancient philosophy. She published on Aristotle, and her dissertation was on Plato. She graduated in 1976, and picked up her MFA in fiction along the way, in 1973. While finishing her dissertation work Peggy was offered a one-year position at the University of Utah. It was not an ideal situation as it meant leaving her family and "basically teaching all the courses nobody else wanted to teach." Given the sorry state of the academic job market at the time, her faculty considered this a boon and pressed her to take it. She did. She was assigned to be one of about two dozen faculty leading sections of Intellectual Traditions survey courses. These faculty gathered periodically, and it was here that she first encountered the man who would become the love of her life, Dr. Brooke Hopkins. She admits now that she was distracted by some of the older, "deadwood" professors at these meetings, so "I didn't notice the really cute guy over here at the other end of the table. But he apparently noticed me. The rest is history."

The first present Brooke gave to Peggy was a collection of Montaigne's essays. "That's how you know that this is an interesting person," she told me. "It wasn't a bunch of flowers...It was wonderful." They traveled the world and their own backyards, hiking and biking through the foothills, camping and exploring the roads and rivers of Utah and beyond. In the meantime, Peggy's one-year position was extended for another year, but she knew she would have to start thinking long term. She applied for a prestigious National Endowment for the Humanities (NEH) fellowship, which she won. Her goal for the fellowship was to write a comprehensive historical monograph on the ethics of suicide (Battin 1982). No one else had touched this issue, and it was a big enough deal that the University of Utah changed her position title from contingent faculty to tenure track. She bought a house with Brooke, eventually married, and they lived there together until his death in 2013.

Becoming a Bioethicist

When I asked Peggy how she turned her philosophy career from Plato to bioethics, she indicated that it is hard to pin down precisely, "It's not as though you wake up one day and say, 'Well, I was doing ancient philosophy, but starting today I'm a bioethicist.' It doesn't work that way."

The start was probably the *Ethics of Suicide* book she completed for the NEH fellowship, which of course was motivated by her mother's big question:

> The proposal I wrote for this fellowship was on ethical issues in suicide. Because there was *nothing*. It was interesting to me. And again, this goes back to the death of my mother. So when she said, "Why should it be so hard to die?" And people were saying, "It's just a little downturn. You'll be up and well by spring." My take away from that was, this is an intelligent woman. Shouldn't she have the right to make whatever choices she wants about how she dies, instead of just being moved along in the standard progression?

In bioethics language, *The Ethics of Suicide* addressed issues related to autonomy in matters of dying. In writing the book, she was breaking new ground and also educating herself:

> I got interested in what kind of choice this woman, my mother, would have made. And of course I don't know. But it seemed to me that she should have had a choice about how to die. The issue about having a choice in how you die has been central to me all along. And that's where it comes from. So I thought, I kept thinking, "Well, how would you describe what another choice might have been?" And that's how I got interested in issues about suicide...She was dying of cancer. Would she have chosen to end her life? I don't know. But it seemed to me, given what a cancer death is like, or can be like, she should have had this choice. So then I thought, you know, there's really nothing to read. There was no contemporary philosophy about this. There was no field of bioethics...So what is there to read? Well, there's Plato, there's Aristotle, there's the Stoics. And these are all the people I had learned about...the early Church fathers, the Medievals, Augustine, Aquinas, and then the Moderns, you know, Hume, Kant, Mill, all those, Nietzsche. So there was nothing [new] to read. Those were the only things to read. So I'd get interlibrary loan to bring me books, and I'd Xerox them...There wasn't any Web, so you couldn't call it up...but this was all based on these historical sources, because there was nothing else to read.

In these early days, there were no bioethics journals, no organizations, no annual conferences. The first bioethics textbook, *Moral Problems in Medicine* (Gorovitz et al. 1976), included a mélange of philosophical and medical topics in a variety of formats. The editors had a difficult time finding a publisher: The publishers they approached all said, "Well, we can't publish this because there aren't any courses called 'bioethics,' so how can we market it?" After many rejections they went back to the first publisher they had tried, Prentice Hall, who finally agreed to take it; the book rapidly became a best seller. Now that a textbook existed, there could be courses. With courses, you could develop a field. Bioethics was a thing.

In the following years, Peggy continued to publish on a variety of bioethics topics. Unwilling to become an armchair philosopher, she traveled the world, visiting with physicians, and developing a method called "oppositional collaboration," in which a bioethics researcher co-conducts empirical work with a researcher who comes at it from the other "side" of things. For example, she and a Catholic nun conducted interviews together while investigating the Netherlands' liberal physician-assisted suicide and euthanasia policies (See Battin 2005). Despite her openness to others' views, Peggy has been unwavering in her position that "A person should be accorded the right to live his or her life as they see fit (provided of course that this does not significantly harm others), and *that includes the way they end their life*" (Battin 2010, p. 403, italics mine).

On November 14, 2008, Peggy's life trajectory shifted dramatically when her husband Brooke Hopkins broke his neck in a bicycle accident, rendering him quadriplegic. Afterward, he was left with essentially zero function below the neck, but completely lucid. His bicycle helmet—a $30 investment—prevented brain damage. Peggy gives her perspective on that day and the early days after the accident below:

> I often went biking with Brooke…But I had a little cold so I went to lectures in the Philosophy department instead…So when I finally came home, and you see a policeman standing outside the door…You *knew* that something had happened to Brooke, because I had been trying to phone. I could tell from the policeman's body language that he wasn't dead, but that something terrible had happened…And so your initial reaction is it is so [*sigh*] completely assaulting, you might say. All your effort is to try to think rationally. How do I get to the hospital?… And then you're so caught up in everything that [*sigh*] it's not that no self-reflection goes on. It's just that the demands, the urgency of the situation is so huge. Will he survive? He'd had probably what would be called walking pneumonia, but with a high spinal cord injury…you lose diaphragm function. But that meant he had to be on a ventilator…What we understood from the doctors was the likelihood of survival was always in question in these

> early days. So it's just hanging on by your fingernails. And then things lengthen out after a while. And then the issue is less clearly about will he die, but will there be any return of function…But you don't know for five weeks or so. So there's this weird period where he's still in the hospital, you can't tell what the outcome is going to be—But it was just *amazingly* demanding.

Brooke never did recover function. He remained almost completely paralyzed from the shoulders down, in what has been described by others as "an inert sack of a body" (Henig 2013a), a description he and Peggy both resisted. An elaborate high-tech assemblage of equipment kept him alive, including a feeding tube, ventilator, diaphragmatic pacer, external oxygen, and a pacemaker. He spent approximately two years in a long-term acute care facility before coming home to Peggy. His house was fitted with new ramps and an elaborate pulley system so he could be transported from his bed to his wheelchair. Twelve caregivers were hired to cover round-the-clock care in a former guest room that had become, in essence, a very small private hospital. And yet there were so many reasons to keep fighting for each day—a "sublime and extraordinary" outpouring of love from friends and family, opportunities to teach and write again, more deeply engaging conversations with Peggy, occasional trips to museums and concerts, walks (in his huge motorized wheelchair) with friends. Brooke was, for the most part and on most days, happy to be alive. There were even times when he said he loved his life. But there were also experiences of deep depression when Brooke told Peggy that he wanted to die.

Meaningful Experiences: Impact on Academic Work

Peggy describes some of the most engaging academic writing she's ever done as taking place while curled up next to Brooke in his bed after the accident. Brooke had a strapping athletic build, and at six foot five inches, he was too tall for a traditional hospital bed. The only bed that could accommodate him was a bariatric bed designed for obese patients. One upside of this arrangement was that the extra width permitted Peggy to crawl into bed alongside him. She would often bring her computer, and they would puzzle through problems confronting them together. Peggy had started a blog as a way to keep friends and family informed in the early days after Brooke's accident, and this gradually morphed into their shared intellectual and emotional outlet.

Brooke's field was romantic poetry, so the blog sometimes referenced Wordsworth and Keats. They also worked together on bioethics problems and new interests, like sex and the male gaze from the perspective of a man who is paralyzed. This writing served an important purpose for these two scholars in that it provided space for the intersection of their intellectual interests and their personal lived experience related to these interests. Peggy describes the blog's meaning below:

> The first word that comes to mind is *bonding*. It's not that we weren't already bonded. This was a really wonderful marriage …And of the things we liked to do together, we loved to travel and hike and do all that stuff, but we were always talking about issues. After the accident we could still do that, except that it was something much more deeply personal and compelling and horrifying in some ways.

Keeping the blog also helped them to work through some bioethics issues from their new insider perspective. Peggy describes her thinking below:

> Since I'd always worked in bioethics I knew quite a lot about medicine generally, and about how information is presented and modulated, and how risk is framed, and about the culture of hospitals, and higher goals, strategies, and the shape of institutions, because I'd been around that all this time. And then to be the patient and the patient's principal family member is—and every doctor who's ever been sick says the same thing, "I never really understood it until *I* was the patient." So suddenly you're on the receiving end of this. You recognize it intellectually, but it *feels* different. It feels—Well it has a much greater reality, because it's not just about somebody else out there who's broken their neck. It's about *you*. You, too, right? I mean both of you. It really is about both of you because while only one has the paralysis, the impact is on the two of you. And part of it is trying to fully understand what this can be like for him. This is somebody you love, right? What can this be like for somebody whose life has always been both intellectual and physical, and who has always had extremely robust health? …He was a guy who enjoyed being out of doors, roaming around the mountains, exploring things, biking everywhere.

Peggy also wrote an audaciously personal piece for the journal *Medicine, Health Care and Philosophy*, which was published two years after Brooke's accident. This article, called "The Irony of Supporting

Physician-Assisted Suicide: A Personal Account," describes the intellectual and emotional tension resulting from the intersection of the personal and the professional. Referencing Dostoevsky's character Ivan Ilych, she asked, "What if my whole life has been wrong?" (Battin 2010, p. 404). In an oft-quoted passage, she acknowledged the new challenges:

> Much of my entire career in writing and thinking about physician-assisted suicide was now on the line. All that academic prose—wheelbarrows of it, it seems—had come under horrifying challenge from life itself. I said I did not know what I'd do if I reread everything I'd written on this topic, but I'm sure that part of me would want to tear it all up.

Peggy's "wheelbarrows" quote is sometimes misinterpreted to mean that after Brooke's accident she changed her mind about end-of-life decision making. She most definitely did not do this. Rather, she saw the issues in finer detail. I asked Peggy to elaborate:

> When you work on an issue, you sort of formulate a position. You see the autonomy issues this way. The conclusion is, yes, people should be entitled to make this choice. That's not to say how they should make it, but it should be open to them. And of course you know *intellectually* all the objections about depression, and the way one's choices are clouded by pain, and what about pressures, and what about institutional incentives?… But now you get to see something about how *real* those things are. What's real, what's not real. And it became more complicated.

The complications Peggy experienced from the intimate position of Brooke's bedside revealed new difficulties with crafting legislation, something she often helps with. At the time of our interview, she was currently assisting a state legislator in the development of a new bill, and this was colored by her experiences with Brooke:

> As you get more involved in the political sphere, there isn't much room for complexity… So you can play a little role in how the law is written… And since I know the person who's running the bill, you can have some say in how she and her legislative people craft the bill. This one makes, for instance, pressuring someone to request assistance by a person, a doctor, an institution, a first-degree felony. That's pretty strong teeth, right? And it's put there to try to persuade people that abuse is unlikely. But the

> texture of individual situations—What counts as pressuring? What counts as trying to persuade somebody? Because there's no situation that is free from people whose views are one way or another. So for instance, and this is back to the personal. In Brooke's case, right from the beginning there was one family member…who I read as clearly thinking that it would be better off if he'd actually been killed. And that I think had to do with the fact that they knew somebody who had a similarly impairing accident, and were aware of how difficult it was for that person, how difficult it was for the family members. But for everybody else the pressure is, "Wow! You're still alive! Keep going!" Those are all pressures in one direction. All those pressures are in favor of continuing. And that included me, right? I was certainly in favor of continuing, even when you see the really hard stuff at close range. I think when it got closer to the end and things were much more difficult for Brooke, it changed in that some—I think most of his friends, the people around him, understood that it was closer to the end, and they were supportive of his choice. There were a couple of people who wanted him to want to keep going. That's the kind of fine-textured stuff that when you're talking public policy, about a bill that has a provision in it about pressures—*how in the world* can you translate that into the actual complexity of real life? We all influence each other all the time about everything. Sometimes it's deliberate and sometimes its unconscious and sometimes it only reflects our own desires.

This intimate understanding of complexity has also made Peggy much more reluctant to generalize in her academic writing. "I didn't change my mind about whether people should have options," she told me, but "I think I *did* come to see that it's *immensely* more complicated…When you talk about it in an academic way…you're not in a position to do fine grained thinking about how different people are." During our interview she elaborated on the importance of acknowledging the difference between her anecdotal experience and the generalizations to which we are inclined in academia:

> My experience is still anecdotal in the sense that it's about the experience of one person, who was in many ways, a remarkable person. So his experience, in spite of all the pain and suffering, was I think still *dramatically* better than that of many other people. So for somebody who, say, was a natural pessimist, or somebody whose social skills, or capacity for social interaction was more limited, or for somebody who was completely self-absorbed, this would be a lot worse for, I think. But of course…I've *met* a lot of people, spending all this time in hospitals, and meeting other people

> with spinal cord injuries, but I realize I can't see it through their eyes the way I can see this one case. So I think the temptation would be to resist generalization more. That goes on in all kinds of writing, you know…It's the nature of what we do. But generalization seems *especially* inappropriate here.

Brooke's Decision to Die

Approximately five years after the accident, and after a year of reflecting on the question, Brooke came to the conclusion that it was time to die. His body was deteriorating rapidly and he was having great difficulty fighting off repeated infections. More devastating, it was becoming much harder to express his thoughts, and he was unsure he could sustain the academic work he was doing from his wheelchair and bed. His refuges were disappearing. He called dear friends and out-of-state family to summon them home. Then he visited his physician to make the official request to have all life supporting technology turned off or removed. Peggy asked the physician to conduct blood tests to make sure Brooke's decision was not due to an undiagnosed infection that could cloud his thinking, as this had happened in the past. She was hopeful that this might be the case, but Brooke's bloodwork came back clear.

Two days later, a hospice physician and nurse arrived at Brooke and Peggy's home. They asked Brooke when he would like his life supporting technology to be withdrawn. He said, "today." Since it would take a few hours to assemble the medications and additional team members, Peggy suggested that the withdrawal take place the next day—she was grasping at anything that could prolong their time together. Unlike Brooke, she was not yet ready to let go. Brooke, however, was firm. He wanted to die today. The medical team agreed on 3:00 pm. A *New York Times Magazine* reporter described the rest of that day:

> With several hours before 3:00, Brooke phoned some old friends to say farewell and then remembered one preparation he had not yet made: choosing a headstone for the gravesite he and Peggy had picked. So he, in his motorized wheelchair, followed by an entourage of family members, respiratory therapists and other caregivers, and close friends went off to the Salt Lake City Cemetery and the little monument company next to it, just a few blocks away, on what was later dubbed the Hopkins Liberation March, to buy a headstone, one for Brooke and one, eventually, for Peggy. They did….And then everyone assembled again at the house. The hospice

> physician gave Brooke a sedative, and Brooke sat in his wheelchair for a while with his stepchildren, his friends, a few of his favorite caregivers and his wife. He said he was getting sleepy, and he was put into bed. Peggy got in beside him. A gospel song he had chosen for the occasion, Marion Williams's "My Soul Looks Back" played on the stereo. Peggy nestled into Brooke's shoulder as the ventilator was dialed down and the morphine and other medications for anxiety and air hunger were delivered so he wouldn't feel like he was strangling. "I lay there and could hear his breathing rate get slower, less regular", [Peggy said], "A breath and then a space, and then a breath and then a long space, a breath and then a very long space."…After the breath that turned out to be the last, Peggy…lay next to Brooke for a very long time, her hand on his face, feeling the warmth leave his body. (Henig 2013b)

In an interview with Terry Gross for National Public Radio (NPR), Peggy described the impact of this moment on her academic work:

> To have it become so real, that someone you love…deeply would be enmeshed in the same…very kind of choice you had been thinking about academically for so long is an extraordinary experience. In one way, it's a healthy experience as it forces me to rethink everything. And even doing that, and even given the acute agony of being so close to something that is so difficult, it doesn't change my basic position that people should…have the right to…be the architects of their own lives, and that includes the very…ends of their lives. You shouldn't have to lose those rights just at the end, especially since the very end makes the greatest amount of difference to some people, and also to some of their loved ones around them. (Gross et al. 2013)

Margaret Pabst Battin Inside the "Well-Lit, Warm Room"

As with the cases of Gillian, Jesse, and Ron, I asked Peggy to read Frankl's quote about his vision of standing at the podium in the well-lit, warm, and pleasant lecture room giving a talk about the concentration camp after the war (reproduced for readers in Chapter 1). Did she see herself at that podium? Peggy immediately saw parallels, in that both she and Frankl had formulated their intellectual stances prior to some of their intimate experiences with suffering and death; Frankl developed logotherapy before entering the camps, and Peggy was an advocate for self-determination in the manner and timing of death before Brooke's accident and his eventual choice to have his life end. She believed that in both her case and Frankl's, personal lives served as affirmations of conclusions drawn, at least in part, through academic work.

Viktor Frankl is best known as a psychiatrist, but he was also a philosopher, having earned a Ph.D. in philosophy in 1949, subsequent to his M.D. in 1930. Peggy is the only philosopher participating in this book project, so I took advantage of a unique opportunity during our interview. I asked her to look through a philosophical—rather than psychological—lens when responding to Frankl's well-lit, warm, and pleasant lecture room metaphor. What would a twenty-first-century philosopher say about it?

> What does the philosopher say?...Can you distance yourself from your immediate environment? Is your intellect powerful enough to make this move? Let me stand back from what's happening. Let me view it objectively as an outsider, not as the person affected. So my guess is...that different people have different capacities to do this. Some people can. Some people can't. It might have been easier for Frankl because he'd worked so much, presumably, with people in getting them to, I assume, see their situations more objectively, and in a less enmeshed or entangled way... So that's what he's doing here...What would a philosopher have to say about it? Well, of course a moral philosopher, somebody doing ethics... and ethics is mostly should we or shouldn't we do stuff like this—[would ask], is this a defensible move to be making? Is the strategy of distancing oneself from what one is actually undergoing a morally decent thing to do, or should you refrain from this device, this self-protective device?...It seems to me that the capacity to do this is impressive and fabulous. And the outcome, that is, [Frankl] bringing this to the entire world, is also impressive.

Peggy did, however, acknowledge that what helped Brooke the most in the midst of his tragedy was not self-distancing, but rather his capacity to stay in the moment, however brutal many aspects of that moment might have been. This strategy came from the wise counsel of a visiting Buddhist teacher, and Brooke's own study of Buddhism undertaken in his forties. During our interview, Peggy reflected how these mindfulness techniques might apply to *our* present moment. We were sitting together at a table in front of a large, sunny window, a copy of Frankl's book *Man's Search for Meaning* (Frankl 1946/2014) in front of us:

> And in a way that's the opposite of [Frankl's self-distancing], but it was among the most helpful of the various kinds of advice [Brooke received]. Live the in present, but try to find the positive features of it in that moment. And after you try to do that a little bit, you'd say, "Well, there's this, you know, horribly injured man in the bed back there" (if this were still then), "but the positive feature is that I'm sitting here talking with somebody I haven't met before, and enjoy." Even though the terrible thing has happened, there's this positive aspect. [*She looks up at a window near us.*] Or the sun is shining on a page from Viktor Frankl. It seems totally trivial, but it's a way of saying, "Look! [she picks up Frankl's book], I didn't know this passage. Not only did I not know it, but the sun is shining on it in a way that illuminates it." That's a different move from what's going on in here [indicates Frankl's quote about the well-lit, warm and pleasant lecture room]... But there's a lot of wisdom in this. It's an exaggerated statement I think. ...I'm trying to think back about whether this is something that I found myself doing, to step back from what's actually happening, and to try to intellectualize something, or to objectify something as a defense mechanism. I'm sure I did. And writing about it, of course, is partly that.

Conclusions

Peggy and I closely scrutinized her vita and the ongoing projects stacked on her dining table to see if her bioethics work had changed direction since Brooke's accident and subsequent death. We came to the conclusion that not much has changed. What makes this difficult to discern is that Peggy has always had a variety of interests within the field of bioethics. Other than the autoethnographic *Irony* piece (Battin 2010), we found one jointly authored book-in-progress, *Puzzles About Disability*, which might have connections with Brooke's accident. But that is all. What is clear is (1) her experience with Brooke did not change her mind about the importance of personal autonomy in matters of death, and (2) her academic work did not take a dramatic new turn after the accident toward issues closely related to her experience with Brooke; she had already been working on those issues beforehand. Rather, her academic concern with these issues intensified and deepened. She acknowledges a new empathy, a reluctance to generalize, and a deeper appreciation for nuance and complexity in end-of-life decision making. This has resulted in new questions about writing legislation that takes into account this complexity and nuance.

As a founder in the field of bioethics, Peggy Battin was uniquely qualified to share Brooke's journey when he chose the manner and timing of his death. As wife of Brooke and daughter of Margaret Richards Pabst, she is also uniquely qualified to write and publish about the bioethical complexities of end-of-life decision making. The unusually personal motivation for her scholarship has origins in personal lived experience—with all its messiness and nuance, but it is informed by the precise and exacting logical and ethical constructions, methodologies, and habits of mind derived from a professional life lived in the intellectual realm. Like Viktor Frankl—and like Gillian, Jesse, and Ron before her—she has found her place in the well-lit room.

I knew from media accounts that Brooke Hopkins was buried in the Salt Lake City cemetery, within easy walking distance of Peggy's home. Before my trip, it occurred to me that I should visit the site and pay my respects to the other great scholar who was helping me with this project. By my second day with Peggy, however, I no longer wanted to do this. Now that I had spent so much time listening to her with such protracted concentration, I had become emotionally invested in her story, and in Brooke. As Kathleen Gilbert points out in *The Emotional Nature of Qualitative Research* (2001), Western research epistemologies view the presence of emotions in the researcher negatively because they put reason and logic at risk. Quite honestly, at this point I was afraid I would cry at Brooke's gravesite and lose any semblance of empirical disinterest. I am not good at faking professional detachment.

Peggy did not forget the original plan, however, and we paid our visit just before I left for the airport. There were some flowers at the site, and Brooke's grave was decorated with little stones left by Jewish friends who had come by on other days.[1] Predictably, I cried. Peggy was gracious, reminding me "Your whole project is about how researchers can have hearts, right?" As we wound our way away around the asphalt roadway from the site, we spied a herd of about a dozen deer sleeping and resting among the monuments, in the shade of some evergreens. Neither of us had ever seen anything like this before. A fitting send-off for a remarkable trip.

[1] It is customary for Jewish visitors to leave stones on graves instead of flowers. Explanations for the origins of this practice vary, but in the present day, it carries meanings relating to respect and remembrance.

Peggy Battin's Advice for Graduate Students Considering Unusually Personal Scholarship

- Advice is often not very helpful. If you want advice, get it from diverse sources. But don't take any of it as directive. Think through your options. Pick the advice that most resonates with you.
- Work on something that is deeply interesting to you. So many students base their scholarship on their perceptions of what's hot in the job market. That's a mistake. You will do more, and do it better, if there is a deeper engagement. So do what interests you.
- Work backward from the way it is usually done in academia. Do your thinking first. Start your work by formulating your ideas on paper so you don't lose them. It doesn't have to be organized. It doesn't have to be in perfect English. It doesn't have to be thorough. And it certainly doesn't have to have footnotes!
- Read the existing scholarship second. If you read everything in the literature first, you will formulate your understanding in other people's terms. We all see things differently, but as soon as you read somebody else's view, you see it their way.
- Aristotle's advice was that you shouldn't aim for happiness. You can't; happiness doesn't work that way. You have to aim at doing something else that's significant, and happiness will come as a by-product of that. So forget about aiming for happiness. Do meaningful work, something you think is important and worth doing, something that will make the world a better place, and you're more likely to be happy in your career.

References

Battin, M. P. (1982). *Ethical issues in suicide.* Englewood Cliffs, NJ: Prentice Hall.

Battin, M. P. (1994). *The least worst death: Essays in bioethics on the end of life.* New York: Oxford University Press.

Battin, M. P. (2010). The irony of supporting physician-assisted suicide: A personal account. *Medicine, Health Care and Philosophy, 13*(4), 403–411.

Battin, M. P., Rhodes, R., & Silvers, A. (Eds.). (1998). *Physician-assisted suicide: Expanding the debate.* New York: Routledge.

Battin, P. (2005). Empirical research in bioethics: The method of oppositional collaboration. In *Ending life: Ethics and the way we die* (pp. 316–320). New York: Oxford University Press.

Frankl, V. E. (1946/2014). *Man's search for meaning*. Boston: Beacon Press.

Gilbert, K. (2001). *The emotional nature of qualitative research*. New York: CRC Press.

Gorovitz, S., Jameton, A. L., Macklin, R., O'Connor, J. M., Perrin, E. V., St. Clair, B. P., et al. (Eds.). (1976). *Moral problems in medicine*. Englewood Cliffs, NJ: Prentice Hall.

Gross, T., & Miller, D. (Producers), & Shorrock, R. (Director). (2013, July 25). For bioethicist with ailing spouse, end-of-life issues hit home [Radio broadcast]. In *Fresh Air*. Philadelphia, PA: National Public Radio.

Henig, R. M. (2013a, July 21). A life-or-death situation. *New York Times Magazine*, p. SM27.

Henig, R. M. (2013b, August 21). Choosing to die after a struggle with life. [Blog] *The 6th Floor: Eavesdropping on The Times Magazine*. Available at: https://6thfloor.blogs.nytimes.com/2013/08/21/choosing-to-die-after-a-struggle-with-life/.

Quill, T., & Battin, M. P. (Eds.). (2004). *The case for physician-assisted dying: The right to excellent end-of-life care and patient choice*. Baltimore: Johns Hopkins University Press.

PART II

Epistemology and Ethics

CHAPTER 6

Introduction to Part II: Franklian Existential Psychology

My life has meaning because of my goal.
—Ronald Mallett, Theoretical Physicist, 2017

This chapter will survey the major themes in Viktor Frankl's existential psychology (also called "logotherapy"), highlighting the anthropological and philosophical assumptions relevant to an exploration of unusually personal scholarship. It is important to note that a complete tutorial in Franklian thought is beyond the scope of this chapter; for instance, I will not discuss the clinical applications of the theory as it applies to psychiatry, counseling, or psychotherapy. Readers can find this in many other sources. Instead, I will draw attention to how Franklian existentialism functions as a psychologically healthful worldview with implications for (1) the Case Study participants from Part I, (2) readers who have unusually personal connections to their scholarship, and (3) the rest of us who want to live meaningfully as teachers and scholars in academic settings. As it turns out, these implications are the same. You do not have to suffer the death of a loved one or be atypically gendered to discover meaning through your scholarship. Logotherapy can benefit anyone.

This inclusive perspective is entirely consistent with the timbre of Frankl's writings, for he was a philosopher as well as a physician (having earned a Ph.D. in philosophy in 1949, subsequent to his M.D. in 1930), and his publications emphasize the broad generalizability of

A. Esping, *Epistemology, Ethics, and Meaning in Unusually Personal Scholarship*, https://doi.org/10.1007/978-3-319-73718-8_6

his theories. Readers interested in a more comprehensive treatment of Franklian existential psychology are encouraged to read (in this order) *Man's Search for Meaning* (1946/2014), *The Will To Meaning* (Frankl 1969/2014), and *The Doctor and the Soul* (1955/1986). The Viktor Frankl Institute of Logotherapy in Abilene, Texas, also has a distance learning curriculum leading to associate and diplomate credentials (http://logotherapyinstitute.org/Home.html). Both the Viktor Frankl Institute of Logotherapy and the International Network on Personal Meaning (INPM) (http://meaning.ca/) sponsor academic conferences.

Viktor Emil Frankl (1905–1997) is best known as the author of *Man's Search for Meaning* (1946/2014), an autobiographical description of his experiences as a psychiatrist imprisoned in four concentration camps during the Second World War. The original edition, published in German in 1946, has in the intervening years been translated into dozens of languages, selling millions of copies worldwide. Many colleges and universities have designated it Book of the Year, and a 1991 survey conducted by the Library of Congress named the English translation one of the "ten most influential books in America." Viktor Frankl Institutes, Libraries, and Centers have also been established in many countries around the world.

Man's Search for Meaning is not a scientific publication. It was written for a wide audience, and its reputation is built on the author's lived human experience, rather than on an appeal to authority based on Frankl's professional qualifications. Indeed, Frankl originally intended to publish *Man's Search for Meaning* anonymously, using his prisoner number only. He was ultimately persuaded to use his name because it was important for him to "have the courage to state [his] convictions openly" (Frankl 1946/2014, p. 6). He was both a psychiatrist and neurologist, serving as Professor of Neurology and Psychiatry at the University of Vienna Medical School and head of the Vienna Neurological Policlinic. He held professorships at several universities, among them Harvard and Stanford. In subsequent years, he received 29 honorary degrees from universities on five continents. His numerous awards include the Oskar Pfister Award of the American Psychiatric Association, the John F. Kennedy Star, and the Albert Schweitzer Medal.

Frankl's preferred term for his existential psychology was "logotherapy," although he occasionally used the labels "existential analysis" and "logotheory." Since his death, his ideas are sometimes called "Franklian existential psychology" or simply "Franklian psychology."

The application of his theoretical ideas to has also been dubbed "logo-analysis" by Crumbaugh and Henrion (2004). Logotherapy remains the most popular term, but I have chosen the designation "Franklian existential psychology" because it highlights the existentialist roots of Frankl's thinking while also de-emphasizing the clinical focus present in many other publications. I want readers to recognize that Frankl's theory has implications for every scholar, and I think the "therapy" part of the term "logotherapy" might be misleading for some who were not already familiar with Frankl's work.

Definitions and Assumptions

Franklian existential psychology is complex even when it is properly understood, but its difficulty is compounded by many philological challenges brought about by inappropriate and inconsistent English translations of key concepts,[1] and Frankl's own adoption of expressions and words that have multiple possible meanings. Given these complications, it seems especially appropriate to begin with some definitions and clarifications.

First it must be understood that Franklian psychology is an existential psychology. At the most basic level, the term "existential" refers to existence, or more specifically, to human existence (Simpson and Weiner 1989). It comes from the Latin *ex* meaning "out of" and *sistere*, which means to "emerge" or "stand out." Any definition beyond this very general one is open to debate, because the thinkers who are usually united under the existential banner are a very diverse group. The situation is further complicated because the words "existentialism" and "existentialist" have become obfuscated through overgeneralization. In a famous speech, the Existentialist philosopher Jean-Paul Sartre (1905–1980) lamented, "Most of those who are making use of this word [existentialism] would be highly confused if required to explain its meaning. For since it has become fashionable, people cheerfully declare that this musician or that painter is 'existentialist.'...and, indeed, the word is now so loosely applied to so many things that it no longer means anything at all"

[1] For example, the English title of *Der Unbewusste Gott* (Frankl 1948) is *The Unconscious God* (1975). This is misleading. In order to remain faithful to Frankl's intended meaning, the translation "God of the Unconscious" would be a closer approximation of his intent (Ann V. Graber, personal communication, November 12, 2004).

(Sartre 1946/1975, p. 347). We can be grateful that Frankl provided his operational definition of the term: He used it "to refer to (1) existence itself, i.e., the specifically human mode of being; (2) the meaning of existence; and (3) the striving to find a concrete meaning in personal existence, that is to say, the will to meaning" (Frankl 1946/2014, p. 94).

Logotherapy

This "will to meaning" is essential for understanding how unusually personal scholarship functions for those who are engaged in it. To get at this, we first have to understand Frankl's preferred term for his existential psychology, "logotherapy." The original Greek word *logos* has many possible interpretations. Heraclitus, Plato, and Aristotle used *logos* in various ways to signify some sort of cosmic order or reason (Blackburn 1996). In Christian theology, it is often translated as "Word" or to designate the second person of the Trinity (Simpson and Weiner 1989). In some discussions, *logos* refers to word and to logic or reason simultaneously. Several pages could be devoted here to teasing out the intricacies and nuances of how *logos* has been used by various authors in these disciplines, but suffice it to say that readers with a background in theology or philosophy may need to suspend their previous understandings of this root word. In Franklian existential psychology, *logos* is used simply to signify "meaning" and it is not intended to have religious overtones.

Logotherapy is a "meaning-centered psychotherapy" wherein a person is "confronted with and reoriented toward the meaning of his life" (Frankl 1946/2014, p. 92). Thus, the direct translation of logotherapy would be "healing through meaning" (Frankl 2014, p. xviii) or "therapy through meaning" (Fabry 1968/1980). The Oxford English Dictionary offers a concise definition of logotherapy: "An existential type of psychotherapy which maintains that [a person's] mental health depends on awareness of meaning in his life" (Simpson and Weiner 1989).

What Is "Meaning"?

But what is meant by "meaning"? Again, this is a tough concept to pin down, as it is very individual. Take a moment to think about this: What do *you* mean when you say "meaning"? If I were to ask you, "What makes your scholarship meaningful for you?", how would you respond? Your answers likely align with Franklian existential psychology, because one of its central tenets is that meaning is a highly personal endeavor, and the role of any person who is attempting to help another to discover meaning is closer to that of an eye specialist than that of a painter: The logotherapist's role, according to Frankl, is not to paint pretty pictures to show how meaningful things can be created from chaos. Rather, it "consists of widening and broadening the visual field…so that the whole spectrum of potential meaning becomes conscious and visible" (1946/2014, p. 103). Therefore, my role in this section is to broaden the reader's perspective so you can see meanings in your scholarship that may, in fact, already be present.

Very often the meanings people need to discover are directly tied to difficult life experiences. Frankl proposed the concept of the "tragic triad" to acknowledge this. The tragic triad consists of (1) unavoidable pain, (2) irretrievable loss, and (3) guilt (Frankl 1946/2014, p. 129). The Part I Case Studies did not explore the ways in which meaning in scholarship can be derived from one's response to guilt, as the participants' life circumstances did not merit this. However, there are many illustrations in those chapters of meaning being derived from the participants' responses to unavoidable pain and irretrievable loss. An essential point here is the use of the modifiers "unavoidable" and "irretrievable." Gillian, Ron, and Peggy lost loved ones to death. This is an unchangeable fact. They cannot get their loved ones back—the losses are **irretrievable**. Another unchangeable fact: They will grieve for the rest of their lives. They will move forward from their losses, but they will never move on. The suffering is **unavoidable**. As much as we may wish to deny it, this is true for all of us. We do not have control over everything that happens in our lives. Such is the human condition.

But Franklian existential psychology asserts that meaningful—indeed sometimes healing—experiences can come from our chosen **responses** to these unchangeable and painful life circumstances. I think the Case Studies in Part I bear this out:

- Peggy was haunted by her mother's question, "Why should it be so hard to die?" She responded to the challenge of that question by writing books, journal articles, and fiction about personal autonomy in matters of death. In doing so, she helped to launch an entirely new field of study, bioethics. Life came full circle when her gravely injured husband was able to choose the manner and timing of his death.

- To this day, Ron's grief for his father is palpable. He channeled this energy into a Ph.D. in theoretical physics and a lifelong "mission" to discover the mechanisms behind time travel. Following in the footsteps of Albert Einstein, his generation of physicists (among them Stephen Hawking and Kip Thorne), has legitimized this area of study. An intensely personal grief is contributing to the discovery of baffling new properties of the very universe itself. His work has not resulted in a time machine, but he may get to see his father again through the magic of Hollywood.
- Gillian was so moved by her own devastation and ill-treatment by well-meaning others in the aftermath of her son's death that she championed the plight of other bereaved parents by taking on, for a time, the banner of bereavement researcher. This work yielded a dissertation with generalizable insights. Perhaps more important in Gillian's case was the perceived therapeutic impact of the graduate school process on Gillian herself; she may have helped others understand parental grief better, but she most certainly helped herself understand it better.
- Jesse, whose story does not involve a death, was faced instead with the unavoidable pain of being an atypically gendered person in a sometimes judgmental and cruel world. He responded by applying to graduate school and becoming an expert on gender. Now he has a much more nuanced and sophisticated understanding of his own journey, and he is also uniquely positioned to share his expertise in public forums around the country. In helping himself, he is helping others. In helping others, he is helping himself.

In each of these cases, the scholars have added something valuable to the world through their intellectual work, while taking away something valuable for themselves in the process. This is meaningful scholarship. It may also be logotherapy. Think of Frankl's own situation as a concentration camp inmate. He could not change his external circumstances. His physical suffering could not be mitigated by anything over which he had control. Arguably, he could not change aspects of his internal circumstances, as his writings acknowledge ongoing psychological suffering while in the camps. (This is a completely normal human response. It would be odd if he did not feel psychological distress in that situation, regardless of any psychotherapeutic or philosophical insights he possessed.)

However, in response to this unavoidable suffering and countless irretrievable losses, Frankl chose to pilfer scraps of paper and begin reconstructing his stolen manuscript for *The Doctor and the Soul* (1955/1986). This act of defiance, this chosen response to unavoidable suffering and irretrievable loss, was meaningful enough that he credited it, in part, with keeping him alive even as physically stronger men perished:

> I am convinced that I owe my survival, among other things, to my resolve to reconstruct that lost manuscript. I started to work on it when I was sick with typhus and tried to keep awake, even in the night, to prevent a vascular collapse. For my 40th birthday an inmate had given me a pencil stub, and almost miraculously he had pilfered a few small SS forms. On the backs of these forms I scribbled notes that might help me reconstruct *The Doctor and the Soul.* The notes actually served me well when I later started to fulfill my hopes by committing to paper the second draft of that first book, now enriched by the confirmation of my theory in the concentration camps. There, in the camp, I had already drafted an additional chapter on the psychology of the camps. (Frankl 1995/2000, p. 98)

These five cases—Frankl's case and those of the four participants interviewed in Part I of this book—illustrate an essential claim supporting logotherapy:

Good does not come from pain.
Good may come from an individual's chosen response to pain.

It is important to say a bit more about this here, because this claim is easily misunderstood. This is not some trite cliché about making lemonade out of lemons. It is instead an acknowledgment that *the lemons may always be there, sour and caustic, and you may also find an opportunity to make lemonade.* To illustrate: One would never, ever, say to Ron, "It is good that your father died because it led to you making all these important discoveries in theoretical physics." Nor would you try to cheer Jesse by saying, "I'm so glad your mom was cruel to you when you were a child, because now you are giving speeches and helping to make it less likely that other transgender children will be mistreated." While acknowledgment of personal sacrifice for the greater good sometimes happens as a part of meaning discovery, it is not required or even necessarily desirable.

Ron and Jesse will keep their pain (the lemons) even though they responded to it in ways that also have an otherwise positive impact on their lives and the lives of others (the lemonade). This perspective is actually very practical. When confronted by adversity, many ruminate on the question, "Why me?" This doesn't necessarily move us forward, as the answer to this question is very often beyond human grasp. (I mean, why *not* you?) This is why in logotherapy it is often more fruitful to ask "*How* me?" (Barnes 1989). If suffering or loss cannot be avoided, one constructive option is to choose how it will be borne. Case in point: Gillian's son died tragically when he was six years old. She bore this loss by choosing to immerse herself in the study of bereavement, thereby helping others who could not or would not do this. Her approach to healing could be described by others as fitting the ancient archetype of the "wounded healer" (Jackson 2001). In a postscript to the 1984 edition of *Man's Search for Meaning*, Frankl called this "tragic optimism" (1946/2014, p. 129).

Meanings and "Values"

So how do scholars choose? According to Frankl, the discovery of meaning manifests through the realization of three types of "values": creative values, experiential values, and attitudinal values (Frankl 1946/2014). Creative values help people discover meaning through what they **give** to the world. For example, a professor may discover meaning through writing a book, teaching a course, becoming an activist, mentoring young scholars, engaging in important service work, or conducting research that will advance the field. (Does your work feel more meaningful when you do any of these things? Which ones? Could you do more of this?) Frankl was exercising creative values when in the midst of ongoing misery he reconstructed his lost manuscript and held fast to his vision of helping other people by writing and speaking about his experiences in that future "well-lit, warm and pleasant lecture room." This is, of course, the metaphor to which I have been consistently referring in the Part I Case Studies.

In Frankl's case, creative values quite literally helped him to stay alive. Thankfully, those scholars who are reading this book are not likely to face such dire conditions, but you do not need to suffer in order to benefit from realizing creative values. Frankl was very clear about this assertion: Regardless of life circumstances, you can discover meaning by giving something to the world. Personally, I am finding work on the present book to be deeply meaningful, and I am typing this paragraph in a lovely sunroom, drinking delicious coffee, and surrounded by three dogs who are very generous with their affection. As difficult as the writing process can be, I am not suffering. All things considered I have it pretty good! I think the key is that I perceive this project as having the potential to (1) be read by more than just the tiny fraction of other scholars who are interested in the kinds of things I am interested in, and (2) help other scholars feel more fulfilled and happy with their academic careers. Your response will bear this out—or not—of course. But I have worked on other projects that I felt had far less potential to contribute anything of value to readers. For the most part, these manuscripts, largely crafted in my pre-tenure quest to be perceived as someone my university wanted to keep around, are still languishing in my hard drive in various states of incompletion. As "hot" topics they had potential to advance my career, but they did nothing to nurture my soul. I am more productive when I take my soul into consideration, not, as might be the more conventional wisdom, when I disregard it in pursuit of "success."

It may be argued that Gillian, Jesse, Ron, and Peggy also discovered meaning through creative values. It might be helpful to pause here to recall their stories and see if you can identify any instances. What, specifically, did they contribute to their fields of study? How might this act of contributing have positively impacted their mental health? A more technical way to ask these questions is this: In what ways did their scholarship function logotherapeutically through the exercise of creative values? Here are some of my thoughts:

- Gillian's meaningful goal in graduate school was to use scholarship to change how people think about bereavement. This was something she could give to therapists, educators, and other bereaved parents through her research and teaching.
- One of Jesse's meaningful goals in graduate school was using his gender research to improve the medical management of babies who are born intersexed. This is something he could give to physicians, parents, and intersexed individuals through a statistical investigation of the two-sex/gender paradigm.
- Ron wants to give the world a time machine. Each published paper contributes something toward this meaningful goal.

- Peggy wants people to have some say in the timing and manner of their deaths. She traveled to the Netherlands accompanied by a Catholic nun to investigate potential misuses of such a policy. Subsequent publications added key information to philosophical and legislative debates about this personally meaningful issue.

Experiential Values

Experiential values are the second way to find meaning. Whereas the realization of creative values allows people to discover meaning through what they give to the world, experiential values help people find meaning in **what the world gives to them**. For example, a professor may discover meaning when she makes an exciting research discovery, commits to a risky but emotionally fulfilling research agenda, savors the delights of genuine intellectual curiosity, enjoys the fruits of her teaching or mentoring labors, or spends a long lunch discussing research ideas or a good book with colleagues. (Are you taking in meaningful experiences as part of your scholarly life? How could you experience more meaning?)

Gratitude is often placed under the heading of experiential values (Coetzer 1992). This is the most salient emotion I feel for my academic work. As a first-generation college student, I am always hyper-aware of my current privilege, and this makes it harder to become annoyed with some of the inevitable frustrations of modern academic life. Do I feel overwhelmed by service commitments? Most days. Do I worry I'm not publishing enough? Seasonally, aligned with annual report and post-tenure review schedules. Do I stress about being intellectually and emotionally generous with my students in light of everything else that takes my energy? Every day. Do I worry about making sure family time remains a priority no matter what happens at work? Definitely. Am I anxious that I'm not exercising enough because it seems like all I have time to do is write, prepare for classes, or sit in on meetings? Today that happens to be my particular concern. And yet, I am not digging ditches. I am a tenured college professor. And I am, as I said, working from home on a project I love, while drinking coffee and petting my dogs. I will remember this tomorrow when I am in meetings. All. Freaking. Day.

It seems clear that in Frankl's situation in the concentration camps, experiential values worked alongside creative values to help him discover meaning. Recall that he credited the decision to reconstruct his lost manuscript with helping to keep him alive. The manuscript and the associated goal of eventually speaking in the "well-lit, warm and pleasant lecture room" were things he would be giving to the world; in this respect, they represent creative values. However, these future-oriented goals were also giving back to him in the present in the form of something positive to daydream about instead of constantly meditating on the unfathomable misery of his current daily existence. In his books, he also speaks about the ways in which his love for his first wife, and his hope of someday seeing her again, kept him going. These experiential values remained a pathway to meaning in the darkest of his days (Frankl 1946/2014).

Gillian, Jesse, Ron, and Peggy may have also discovered meaning through experiential values. Pause here for a minute and try to identify examples from their Case Studies. What, specifically, did their scholarship give to each of them? How might this act of receiving have positively impacted their mental health? A more technical way to ask these questions is this: In what ways did their scholarship function logotherapeutically through the exercise of experiential values? Here are some possibilities to consider:

- Reading scholarly papers on parental bereavement normalized Gillian's personal experience of grief. Creating literature reviews for courses and publications helped her find language for what she was feeling. This was both meaningful and healing.
- Jesse's public lectures about the two-sex/gender paradigm helped facilitate his coming-out process. He is much more confident and happy because of his deep engagement with gender research in academia.
- Ron's feels "blessed" that he has been able to study physics in his father's honor: "I mean how many people get the opportunity to be paid to study about the universe itself? I mean it's about as close to theology as you can get without being a theologian."
- Some of Peggy's most "deeply engaging" and meaningful academic writing took place while curled up in bed next to her husband as they puzzled through philosophical and bioethical problems.

Attitudinal Values

The third category is attitudinal values. Realization of attitudinal values is usually considered by logotherapists to be the highest form of meaning discovery because these values are available even when access to creative values (giving something meaningful to the world) and experiential values (taking something meaningful from the world) has been limited. As Frankl's tragic triad asserts, some life circumstances, like death or illness, cannot be escaped (Frankl 1946/2014, p. 129). However, **choosing one's response** toward these circumstances can be spiritually liberating. For this reason, Franklian existentialism designates the ability to change one's attitude toward an unchangeable fate as "the last of human freedoms" (Allport 1984, p. 12). (How have you chosen a different attitude toward unchangeable aspects of your life or scholarship? Are there painful aspects of your personal history that could contribute positively—are already contributing positively—to your scholarship? Is there a way to reframe your perception of pain so it becomes purpose?)

Consider again the case of Frankl in the concentration camps. He had very little freedom to make changes to his external circumstances. Nearly, every aspect of his day-to-day existence was chosen for him and ferociously monitored by the SS. He put himself at mortal risk when he took a pencil nub and some pilfered SS forms to begin rewriting *The Doctor and the Soul*. He was also in a devastated physical condition, so even his own body limited his freedom to act. Mental distress arising from his horrific situation also placed certain limitations on his psychological liberty. However, the moment when he recognized his unique opportunity as a psychiatrist in a concentration camp is a powerful example of spiritual freedom. He knew that he could not escape the physical and psychological horrors of his circumstances, but he could use his professional expertise as a psychiatrist to study those circumstances and communicate his findings to the world. This decision had potential to help other people while also helping himself.

Attitudinal values are also present in the Part I Case Studies. Take a moment of reflection to see if you can identify any illustrations from these stories. How did each scholar choose an attitude toward life circumstances she or he could not change? How might these chosen attitudes have positively impacted their mental health? A more technical way to ask these questions is this: In what ways did their scholarship function logotherapeutically through the exercise of attitudinal values? Here are some possibilities to consider:

- Gillian's example of the dogwood tree she planted on the day her son died illustrates how she exercised attitudinal values to find a "purpose" for the distressing thoughts from which she could not escape: "Every spring when I watch it bloom it reminds me of another year without Timothy...It's such a powerful thought to have in your head...But when you write it down... or I...talk about it in lecture it becomes very real. It becomes alive...[It's] very painful for me to watch that [tree] every year...but when I can share it, or I can explain it, or I can give it to somebody else then it doesn't hurt so much. And it has a purpose. That thought has a purpose. It ... helps me to explain to somebody else what it feels like [to grieve]".
- Jesse started graduate school as a closeted transgender person who was fearful of being rejected by his academic peers and faculty. After coming out to a colleague, he recognized that his transgender experience could be used to educate other people through public lectures.
- As Ron got older, he recognized that time travel backward to see his father would not be possible in his lifetime. Despite his lifelong pursuit of this goal, he did not despair. Instead, he said this: "This trying to attain the unattainable...That bittersweet part. I suspected it was going to be there the older I got, and the more I learned about physics. But I knew that was something I still had to go for, because...that's the thing that gave meaning to me in my personal life, was the love that I had for my father, the love I still have for my father..."
- Brooke's accident demonstrated to Peggy the pitfalls of generalizing when writing or legislating about end-of-life decisions. She has chosen to take these new insights and apply them to her academic work. What she generates from this may help other families in their final hours.

Uniqueness and Responsibility

One overall statement that can be defended with regard to all flavors of existentialism is that the philosophical school is preternaturally concerned with issues of the particular, rather than the general (Sanborn 1968). Frankl's take on the particular focuses on (1) the opportunities presented by the inherent uniqueness of every individual, and (2) each individual's responsibility to acknowledge and manifest these opportunities. In

The Doctor and the Soul, he writes, "With his unique destiny each man stands, so to speak, alone in the entire cosmos. His destiny will not recur. No one else has the same potentialities as he, nor will he himself be given them again" (1955/1986, p. 75).

Since each person is unlike anyone else in the world, each individual can contribute to the world in a way that is unique and irreplaceable. This applies to scholars, too. Let's consider what can be learned from Frankl's own experience of uniqueness. At the pivotal moment when he envisioned the "well-lit, warm and pleasant lecture room," Frankl acknowledged that as psychiatrist interned in a concentration camp he was in an exceptional position to field test psychological and philosophical ideas previously put forth by himself and others from the pristine comfort of the ivory tower. His imprisonment provided the perfect natural experiment.

In accepting this opportunity to do what he was perhaps uniquely positioned to do—that is, study the psychology of the concentration camp from the inside—he accepted responsibility (the ability to respond) and transformed it into responsibleness (the act of being responsible). According to Frankl, this responsibleness is the very "essence of existence" (Frankl 2000, p. 29). Frankl's responsibleness in the camps culminated in a singular contribution to the genre of holocaust narrative, *Man's Search for Meaning* (1946/2014), his reconstructed psychological treatise, *The Doctor and the Soul* (1955/1986), and dozens of subsequent publications, public lectures, and university teaching.

Gillian, Jesse, and Peggy are also unique in that they have an insider understanding of phenomena that may contribute to their scholarship and academic insight that may contribute to their self-understanding. This might be conceptualized as a form of identity intersectionality (Crenshaw 1989). The intersectionality of Frankl's personhood as a Jew, a husband, a son, and a prisoner intersected with his professional identity as an academic, a psychiatrist, and a neurologist to create a uniquely holistic perspective that was far more than the sum of its parts: Rather than being different lenses he could use to view his situation, his identities existed in an iterative relationship as "reciprocally constructing phenomena" (see Collins 2015, p. 2). To put it more simply, his unusually personal scholarship contributed more to our understanding of the concentration camp experience than would a scholarly contribution co-authored by an outsider psychiatrist and a prisoner who was not a psychiatrist. By extension, this is also true for Gillian, Jesse, and Peggy.

Another way to look at this unique insider/academic perspective is to interpret it as form of double consciousness. This idea was first described by the historian and sociologist W. E. B. Du Bois to describe aspects of the African American experience (1887, 1903/1994). It has been adopted by some postmodern social scientists for explaining and justifying reflexive forms of ethnography that embrace both the researcher's personal lived experience and her professional training (see Reed-Danahay 1997). This kind of writing capitalizes on the writer's double consciousness as (1) a private human person who experiences the condition from the inside, subjectively, and (2) a professional social scientist who knows how to look at the condition (with varying degrees of objectivity) from the outside. These careful observers are able to shift between identities, "foreground[ing] the multiple nature of selfhood and open[ing] up new ways about writing about social life" (Reed-Danahay 1997, p. 3). As I put it in an earlier publication, this perspective capitalizes on the "unique coincidence in a single individual of two identities, the personal and the professional" (Esping 2011, p. 60).

The existentialist emphasis on the particular in favor of the general also has special relevance to researchers, as the particular-general distinction lies at the core of many epistemological arguments. We will look closely at these issues in Chapters 7 and 8.

Franklian Anthropology

One way to look at any psychological framework is to break it down into its assumptions about what it means to be human. Frankl's claims about what a human being *is* cannot be disentangled from the existential assumptions of his logotherapeutic model. Therefore, the reader should become aware of several anthropological assumptions. As Frankl put it:

> Existential analysis is the attempt at a psychotherapeutic anthropology, an anthropology that precedes all psychotherapy, not only logotherapy. Indeed, every psychotherapy plays itself out against an *a priori* horizon. There is always an anthropological conception at its foundation, no matter how little aware of this the psychotherapy may be. (Frankl 1956/2004, p. 230)

What Is a Human Being?

Human beings exist as a three-dimensional unit: The somatic (body), psychogenic (mind) and noetic ("meaning-seeking") dimensions combine to create an indivisible whole. The first two dimensions are probably familiar to most readers as they take the form of the familiar "mind-body" connection endorsed as a holistic approach to medicine and psychology. The noetic dimension is less easily defined. In Frankl's view, it is that part of us which sets human beings apart from other creatures; it is the "specifically human dimension" (Frankl 1946/2014, p. 95) or "what is human in man" (Frankl 2000, p. 28). It is the inner resource thought to contain the capacity for conscience, creativity, faith, humor, self-detachment, self-transcendence, responsibleness, the search for meaning, and other resources that, according to Frankl, are available only to human beings (Graber 2004). These specifically human resources of the noetic dimension are what clinicians mobilize in logotherapy, and they may also be resources that have the potential to allow scholars to transform elements of the tragic triad into something meaningful.

What Is Human Life?

According to Franklian existential psychology, human life rests on the three pillars:

1. The freedom of will
2. The will to meaning
3. The meaning of life

The freedom of will allows the individual to make choices about how to respond to a given set of life circumstances. Although the somatic and psychogenic dimensions are often irreparably damaged by external and internal circumstances (e.g., a physical illness; grief), the presence of the noetic dimension means that people retain some freedom to move in response to the unchangeable situation. Exercising this freedom requires a degree of self-detachment; that is, the individual must use the resources of the noetic dimension to choose an attitude in regard to the limitations of the psychogenic and somatic dimensions.

As evidence of the freedom to choose even under the most dire circumstances, Frankl told of some starving concentration camp inmates who chose to steal scraps of bread from weaker prisoners. They justified their actions by claiming that the theft victims were going to die soon anyway, while they still had a chance of living. Conversely, other starving prisoners gave away their last scraps of bread to others they perceived as being closer to death—and hence more in need—than they were. As Frankl put it, "faced with the identical situation, one man degenerated while another attained virtual saintliness" (Frankl 1955/1986, p. xxv). The Case Studies in Part I demonstrate some rather heroic examples of scholars exercising their freedom of will. These professors did not degenerate into a chronic state of bitterness and anger (although it would be perfectly reasonable for them to have episodes of this). Instead, they looked beyond themselves at more global problems that they—like Frankl—were perhaps uniquely well-positioned to help solve. For example, Gillian and Jesse both began their scholarship, in part, because they wanted to help people who were being ill-treated by society.

The second pillar, **the will to meaning**, asserts the innate and healthy motivation inherent in all people to search for meaning in life circumstances and to find their purpose(s) on earth. Franklian existential psychology claims that the "ultimate" concerns of human beings, such as questions about the meaning of life, death, and suffering, are the most powerful motivational forces in human beings, surpassing other biological and psychological concerns, including Freud's pleasure principle and Adler's will to power (Frankl 1946/2014). Some support for Frankl's view can come from the Case Studies in Part I: In all four cases, the participants acknowledged that engaging in their unusually personal scholarship is sometimes painful in ways that more typically motivated scholars do not have to experience. Imagine for a second that Peggy's story was about a scholar who saw her husband die, and then ceased her current line of study. This would have been a perfectly understandable, even reasonable, response. But that was not her story. The meanings the participants derived from their scholarly engagement were worth the emotional cost. For example, Gillian described writing papers for her grief courses as simultaneously "therapeutic" and "absolutely draining" emotionally. Speaking publically about bereavement was "terrifying" but also something she "loved." Of course there is an important caveat that she eventually abandoned this research area entirely, finding it ultimately "too painful." The claim that the will to meaning is the most powerful motivator for human beings is controversial and merits a deeper inquiry. Chapter 9 looks closely at Franklian existential psychology as a theory of motivation.

The third pillar, **the meaning of life**, asserts that life circumstances always have meaning potentials, regardless of how tragic, how banal, or how wonderful, they at first appear to be. Practically speaking, it is these dynamic, day-to-day meanings that should concern us; in noetic decision making, it is often more useful to deal with the here-and-now rather than to pose profound questions about the grand, overall meaning of life. Frankl put it this way:

> What matters...is not the meaning in life *in general* [italics mine], but rather the specific meaning of a person's life at a given moment. To put the question [of the meaning of life] in general terms would be comparable to the question posed to a chess champion: "Tell me, Master, what is the best move in the world?" There simply is no such thing as the best or even a good move apart from a particular situation in a game...The same holds true for human existence. One should not search for an abstract meaning of life. Everyone has his own specific vocation or mission in life to carry out a concrete assignment which demands fulfillment. Therein he cannot be replaced, nor can his life be repeated. Thus, everyone's task is as unique as his specific opportunity to implement it. (1946/2014, pp. 101–102)

The moment when Frankl realized he could use his imprisonment as an opportunity to study concentration camp life is an example of this third pillar, as were his daily, risky decisions to record his observations on pilfered scraps of paper. Other examples include Gillian's decision to study parental bereavement, Jesse's choice to study gender, Ron's dogged persistence in finding opportunities to investigate time travel, and Peggy's prolific contributions to developing the brand-new field of bioethics.

Conclusions

This chapter provided an overview of some key themes in Franklian existential psychology as they pertain to the case studies of unusually personal scholarship presented in Part I. A one-page review of this material is provided at the end of this paragraph. This chapter can also be viewed as offering a potentially therapeutic framework for readers who have unusually personal motivations for their own scholarship. Indeed,

I believe that Franklian existentialism can help everyone working in the academy discover more meaning in their endeavors, even if (as is more common) scholarship is motivated by solving problems unrelated to one's own life experience. To this end, this chapter concludes with a set of existential questions for the reader. Remember, Franklian existential psychology supports this claim:

> *A researcher's mental health depends—in part—on an awareness of meaning in her scholarship.*

Review of Franklian Existential Psychology

- Franklian existential psychology has clinical applications, but it is also applicable to the general population. One does not need to be in therapy to benefit from this perspective.
- The most popular name for Franklian existential psychology is logotherapy, which translates to "healing through meaning" or "therapy through meaning."
- Meaning discovery is very individual. Your meaning may not be my meaning.
- Meanings are often discovered as a healthful response to the "tragic triad" of unavoidable pain, irretrievable loss, and guilt.
- You do not need to suffer to discover meaning.
- In painful and unchangeable situations, instead of asking "Why me?", consider asking "How me?" This is "tragic optimism."
- Meaning can be discovered through three types of "values": creative values (what you give to the world), experiential values (what you take from the world), and attitudinal values (choosing your response toward unchangeable circumstances).
- Attitudinal values represent "the last of human freedoms."
- Every person is unique and irreplaceable.
- It is each person's responsibility to manifest opportunities presented by uniqueness.
- Human beings are a three-dimensional unit, consisting of the somatic (body), psychogenic (mind), and noetic ("meaning-seeking") dimensions.
- Human life rests on three pillars: the freedom of will (the ability to make choices), the will to meaning (the inherent desire in all people to search for meaning in their lives), and the meaning of life (the assertion that life always has the potential for meaning).

Existential Questions for Readers

1. What makes your scholarship meaningful for you? (You can define "meaning" however you like.) How could it become more meaningful?
2. Can you identify ways in which you are using your scholarship to realize creative, experiential, and/or attitudinal values? How do these concepts illuminate the presence or absence of meaning in your work?
3. As a scholar, how are you unique? In what ways have you utilized this uniqueness to advance your scholarship? Could you be doing anything differently to use your uniqueness better?
4. Have you ever felt like there are circumstances in your scholarly life that you are not at liberty to change? How might a logotherapeutic perspective help you respond to these constraints in way that brings meaning to the situation?
5. In what ways do you identify with Frankl's vision of standing at the podium in the "well-lit, warm and pleasant lecture room"?

References

Allport, G. (1984). Preface. In V. Frankl (Au.), *Man's search for meaning* (pp. 9–13). New York: Pocket Books.

Barnes, R. C. (1989). Finding meaning in suffering. *The International Forum for Logotherapy, 12*(2), 82–88.

Blackburn, S. (Ed.). (1996). *The Oxford dictionary of philosophy*. Oxford: Oxford University Press.

Coetzer, P. H. (1992). Gratefulness: A highway to meaning? *The International Forum for Logotherapy, 15*, 104–107.

Collins, P. H. (2015). Intersectionality's definitional dilemmas. *Annual Review of Sociology, 41*, 1–20.

Crenshaw, K. (1989). Demarginalizing the intersection of race and sex: A black feminist critique of antidiscrimination doctrine, feminist theory, and antiracist politics. *University of Chicago Legal Forum, 1*, 139–167.

Crumbaugh, J. C., & Henrion, R. P. (2004). *The power of meaningful intimacy: Key to successful relationships*. Indianapolis: Xlibris.

Du Bois, W. E. B. (1887, August). Strivings of the Negro people. *The Atlantic*, p. 197.

Du Bois, W. E. B. (1903/1994). *The souls of black folk*. New York: Dover.

Esping, A. (2011). Autoethnography as logotherapy: An existential analysis of meaningful social science inquiry. *Journal of Border Educational Research, 9*(1), 59–68.

Fabry, J. B. (1968/1980). *The pursuit of meaning: Viktor Frankl, logotherapy and life* (Rev. ed.). San Francisco: Harper & Rowe.

Frankl, V. E. (1946/2014). *Man's search for meaning*. Boston: Beacon Press.

Frankl, V. E. (1948/1975). *The unconscious god*. New York: Simon & Schuster.

Frankl, V. E. (1955/1986). *The doctor and the soul*. New York: Vintage Books.

Frankl, V. E. (1956/2004). *On the theory and therapy of mental disorders: An introduction to logotherapy and existential analysis* (J. M. Du Bois, Trans.). New York: Brunner-Routledge.

Frankl, V. E. (1969/2014). *The will to meaning: Foundations and applications of logotherapy*. New York: Meridian.

Frankl, V. E. (1995/2000). *Recollections: An autobiography* (J. Fabry & J. Fabry, Trans.). Cambridge: Basic Books.

Frankl, V. E. (2000). *Man's search for ultimate meaning*. Cambridge: Perseus.

Graber, A. V. (2004). *Viktor Frankl's logotherapy: Method of choice in ecumenical pastoral psychology* (2nd ed.). Lima, OH: Wyndham Hall.

Jackson, S. W. (2001). The wounded healer. *Bulletin of the History of Medicine, 75*, 1–36.

Reed-Danahay, D. E. (Ed.). (1997). *Auto/ethnography: Rewriting the self and the social*. New York: Berg.

Sanborn, P. F. (1968). *Existentialism*. New York: Pegasus.

Sarte, J. (1946/1975). Existentialism as a humanism. In W. Kaufman (Ed.), *Existentialism from Dostoevsky to Sartre* (pp. 345–369). New York: Meridian.

Simpson, J. A., & Weiner, E. (Eds.). (1989). *The Oxford English Dictionary*. Oxford: Clarendon Press.

CHAPTER 7

Franklian Existential Epistemology

The world is really complex. And we all each only know a tiny part of it. And furthermore we see it through our own eyes. So in a way that's a simplifying feature, because you don't see the complexities. It's like being in a world in black and white.
—Margaret Pabst Battin, Bioethicist, 2017

Franklian existential psychology generates a defensible epistemological framework for unusually personal research, including its most progressive manifestation, autoethnography. Readers with specific interest in autoethnography may find two previous publications (Esping 2010, 2011) helpful complements to the broader perspective provided here.

One controversial characteristic of existentialism, from the standpoint of mainstream research practices at least, is that it embraces subjective experience as an indispensable characteristic of truth. In underscoring the value of individual personal experience, it (gasp!) plays down generalizability and looks instead for the singular human beings "who [have] been hidden in the 'untruth' of the crowd" (Sanborn 1968, p. 18). This emphasis on the particular can be seen in the Perspectivalism of Friedrich Nietzsche, the individualism of Sartre and Kierkegaard, and in Viktor Frankl's focus on meaning potentials inherent in each person's uniqueness.

A. Esping, *Epistemology, Ethics, and Meaning in Unusually Personal Scholarship*, https://doi.org/10.1007/978-3-319-73718-8_7

Epistemology and Individual Uniqueness

Frankl asserted that each human being's uniqueness results from three things: (1) the individual's **disposition**, or natural talents and limitations, (2) the individual's **situation**, or circumstances and environment, and (3) the individual's **positions**, which are the chosen attitudes and/or actions she chooses toward her (potentially unchangeable) disposition and situation (Frankl 1955/1986). With regard to the creation of *Man's Search for Meaning* (1946/2014), relevant dispositions include Frankl's innate talents and limitations as a writer and thinker. His situation was that of a psychiatrist imprisoned in concentration camps. Frankl's decision to begin mental preparation for eventually writing and lecturing about his experience is an example of a position chosen toward the limitations of his unchangeable disposition and situation. The specific interpretations of his camp experiences that he derived from his double consciousness of scientist and sufferer are also manifestations of his positions (see Du Bois 1887, 1903/1994; Reed-Danahay 1997).

This intersection of disposition, situation, and position was a unique combination in Frankl; other individuals shared aspects of his disposition (e.g., talented writers), situation (e.g., psychiatrist/prisoners), and position (decision to write; similar interpretations of events and meanings). However, Frankl would probably have argued that only he could have written *Man's Search for Meaning* (1946/2014). A singular blend of disposition, situation, and position was necessary for that creation to come into being. Thus, its value as a social science text (if that is what it is) would be based on the opportunities derived from the particular, not the general.

Disposition, Situation, and Position in Unusually Personal Scholarship

When scholars begin a dissertation or other potentially publishable manuscript, they bring to the table a host of extant dispositions just because of who they are as unique human beings. These will include any variable that has been invoked as part of the ongoing nature–nurture debate in behavioral genetics,[1] such as their intelligence profile, personality attributes, and physical stamina. Relevant characteristics emerging from

[1] Questions about where these characteristics come from are better conceptualized as being part of "nature via nurture" processes than "nature vs. nurture" debate. See Ridley (2003) for an insightful and very readable overview.

these might include how well they write, how well they deal with being alone for long periods of writing or researching, their ability to sustain focus, and how long they can work at a stretch before needing rest. In the advice Gillian's dissertation Chair provided in Chapter 2 of the present book, she wrote that some personally bereaved graduate students would have been "overwhelmed" by researching parental bereavement, whereas Gillian possessed "the inner strength, sense of mission, and coping methods to carry her through." Gillian was also, in her own words, feeling "depressed," at times "crazy," and "like I am gonna cry forever." This is also part of who she was when she entered her graduate program. Therefore, they are aspects of her individual **disposition**. Some of these dispositions may be changeable, others not.

The Case Studies from Part I can be used to illustrate how disposition, situation, and position interact in unusually personal scholarship. Let's examine each participant in turn.

The most germane aspect of Gillian's **situation** was that she was the mother of a little boy who died when he was six years old. Other relevant features include the presence of an excellent university nearby her home and the fact that a world-class researcher on death, grief, and loss happened to teach there. Her situation also comprised her family makeup (still raising one other child while going through a divorce; extended family living nearby), and the state of her finances (drastically reduced since the divorce), and her painful experiences with well-meaning therapists, friends, and family who seemed to have awkward or inappropriate reactions to her grief. These are features of her immediate context, hence her situation. Some of these conditions are changeable, others not.

Gillian's first **position** toward her disposition (a person who was feeling depressed, but also possessing "inner strength"), and situation (the mother of a dead child, living near a university with a prominent bereavement researcher), was claiming that as an insider, she had something of singular value to contribute to the dialogue about parental bereavement (getting her "voice heard"). Her dissertation, which focused on the experiences of other bereaved parents, is the product of this unique constellation of disposition, situation, and position. And this is what makes it a scholarly contribution that perhaps only she could make. She shared aspects of her disposition with numerous others—there are many other depressed people with inner strength. Her situation is also not entirely unique, as other bereaved people lived within driving distance of her university. Her position—to go to school, learn as much as she could, and then write a dissertation—is a singular manifestation of her will to meaning. And despite the fact that her dissertation findings may be generalizable (transferable), the findings came into being because of the particular; since a Ph.D. dissertation is by definition the creation of new knowledge, it is hard to argue that Gillian's unique humanity did not contribute to this work.

Gillian's second-chosen position, taken after graduate school, was to utilize her disposition (some of which is stable, but some of which evolved as got older, learned more, and moved through her bereavement process and her Ph.D.) and situation (research fellow at an Ivy League university), was to study educational technology. Her published research in this field may seem less connected to her disposition and situation, but this is not the case. It is simply a different position taken toward her circumstances and talents. Recall the sense of relief she articulated with regard to finally studying something that is "fun" with "nothing sad about it." Her enthusiasm for her new area of research is backgrounded by everything else leading up to it. Just as before, she made her professional choice in the context of her disposition and situation. And her new line of scholarship is undoubtedly influenced by these facets of her unique personhood. So it is with all of us who work in the academy.

Jesse completed a dissertation related to gender, but his ongoing scholarly contributions are reflected in the gender talks he gives at universities and other venues around the country. Some relevant aspects of his **disposition** include he is transgender, he is a very precise and linear thinker, and he is a talented and enthusiastic communicator. His **situation** comprises his painful family history, his current appointment as a faculty member in a well-regarded program (proving both cultural capital and a potentially national platform), deep content knowledge (derived from his Ph.D. studies), and heightened public awareness of, and interest in, transgender celebrities. Jesse's chosen **position** with regard to his disposition and situation (some of which he had little control over) is that he is going to "enjoy life." Giving gender talks helps him to do this. Ultimately, he wants to take these talks out of academia and into the mainstream. This position has evolved from that which he articulated in graduate school. In graduate school, his stated position emphasized the role of the academy in his talks and deemphasized his own happiness in favor of his special responsibility to change public perceptions of, and actions toward, atypically gendered individuals.

The divergent positions Gillian and Jesse chose for themselves at different points in their academic journeys highlight the changeable nature of positions taken with regard to one's (potentially unchangeable) talents, limitations, and life circumstances. Ron Mallett's story provides contrast here. One feature of Ron's **disposition** stands out in high relief—his capacity for grit. In recent years, this attribute has emerged in motivation research as an important feature of high achievement in a number of domains. Its definition follows:

> We define grit as perseverance and passion for long-term goals. Grit entails working strenuously toward challenges, maintaining effort and interest over years despite failure, adversity, and plateaus in progress. The gritty individual approaches achievement as a marathon; his or her advantage is stamina. Whereas disappointment or boredom signals to others that it is time to change trajectory and cut losses, the gritty individual stays the course. (Duckworth et al. 2007, pp. 1087–1088)

It is helpful to layer Ron's Case Study over a horizon of grit. This construct permeates every aspect of his journey. From his sustained personal reading regimen in his boyhood to his long hours of study during his Air Force days, through his Ph.D. thesis and ultimately, retirement from a full professorship, he never changed course from the goal he dreamed up as an 11-year-old child. Essential also to his disposition are his high mathematical IQ and his capacity for spatial reasoning. (I did not test him for either of these, but it would be very difficult to become a successful theoretical physicist in the absence of these traits.) The most salient feature of his **situation** was his father's death, but as he grew, it also came to include his access to reading materials from the Salvation Army thrift store, the GI Bill that could pay for college, and ultimately, his full professorship at a major research university. The **position** he took toward his father's death (situation) and his intellectual and motivational dispositions (highly intelligent, gritty) was that he was going to try to build a time machine.

Peggy Battin has also been unwavering in the **position** she chose toward the **situation** of her mother's lingering death. For more than half a century, she has maintained that people should have some autonomy in the manner and timing of their deaths. Taking into consideration her writing ability, her naturally curious and energetic nature, and her penetrating intellect (aspects of her **disposition** I noticed while visiting her), and the situation of her mother's death, her philosophy degrees, and the opportunity to apply for a research fellowship, she chose to begin writing about issues of autonomy in matters of dying. Certainly, other talented philosophers have watched people die slowly. Few of them choose to write about it. Some of them, if asked, would articulate a position diametrically opposed to that which Peggy chose. This shows that the path Peggy took with her scholarship was not an inevitable consequence of her disposition and situation. Like Frankl, Gillian, Jesse, and Ron, she recognized that she had something constructive to offer, given her unique disposition and the difficult context in which she found herself. After her recent experience with her husband's death, she may yet contribute more.

Autoethnography

In the hard sciences, positivism reigns and generalizability is seen as an essential component of the inquiry process. The social sciences are more forgiving, and at present, many epistemological paradigms coexist more or less peacefully. These vary in their stances with regard to generalizability. With existentialism, it is precisely the incommutableness of each scholar's unique combination of disposition, situation, and position that makes her particular academic contribution valuable, but this also means that generalizability may not be possible. This can be perceived by some as threatening the status of unusually personal research as, well, *research*. An excellent illustration is the controversial practice called "autoethnography."

Ethnography (without the "auto" prefix) is a set of mainstream research practices with roots in anthropology. The name comes from the Greek terms *ethnos*, meaning "people," and *grapho*, meaning "I write." Ethnographers utilize a variety of systematic data collection methods and interpretive frameworks from their disciplines to create empirically defensible representations of cultural groups. A classic example most readers will have heard of is Margaret Mead's *Coming of Age in Samoa* (1928/2001). Over many decades, ethnography has been adopted and adapted by multiple social science disciplines, including sociology, psychology, communication studies, political science, and my own field, education. Its practices have also evolved to include a variety of new forms. One of the most controversial iterations is autoethnography. The addition of the Greek root *auto* as the prefix makes it clear what this process involves: self-people-I write.

In autoethnography, the writer uses her personal lived experiences as one lens for interpreting and representing the larger psychological, social, cultural, and/or political worlds shaping and being shaped by these experiences. These works sometimes look like stories, but a careful reading will peel back layers to reveal a recognizable social science foundation. Other times, the personal stories are framed by sections that look like a literature review from a traditional research publication. In other publications, the autoethnographer toggles back and forth between something that looks like mainstream social science and, say, a poem. Some of the most *avant garde* autoethnographies are performances or works of visual art.[2] In these cases, the status of the work as autoethnography may be predicated on the author's professional status as a scholar (see Denzin and Lincoln 2003; Ellis 2004).

Some of my first encounters with autoethnography remain my favorites. I say "favorite" because they are technical masterpieces of the genre. But they are not at all easy reading from an emotional standpoint. They also induce cognitive dissonance and demand ongoing discernment with regard to critical issues of epistemological and ontological[3] validity. In myriad ways, they are complicated, problematic, and at times, lovely. These examples come from an edited volume, *Composing Ethnography: Alternative Forms of Qualitative Writing* (Ellis and Bochner 1996). Culture studies and critical media Professor Lisa Tillmann-Healy's[4] "A Secret Life in a Culture of Thinness: Reflections on Body, Food and Bulimia" (1996) weaves a traditional literature review and theoretical discussion into dramatic scenes from her own struggles with the disorder. In "My Mother is Mentally Retarded," Carol Rambo Ronai[5] layers a sociological perspective on scenes from her life growing up as the offspring of a developmentally disabled mother and her rapist (1996). In "Silent Voices: A Subversive Reading of Child Sexual Abuse," Karen V. Fox visually juxtaposes three accounts of sexual abuse in a single narrative—that of the abuser, the survivor of his abuse, and Fox's own reflections on interacting with these two individuals (1996).

[2] It seems that autoethnography and existential philosophy have in common a shared aesthetic sensibility (Sanborn 1968).

[3] Ontology is the study of the nature of being. Here we are asking, "what is it, really?"

[4] She now uses the name Lisa Tillman.

[5] She now uses the name Carol Rambo.

The anthropologist Deborah Reed-Danahay claims that a fundamental characteristic of autoethnography is boundary-crossing between identities, inasmuch as the author of the piece is constantly shifting between his personal and professional lenses, "foreground[ing] the multiple nature of selfhood" and "open[ing] up new ways of writing about social life." (1997, p. 3). She sees W. E. B. Du Bois' notion of "double consciousness" (1887, 1903/1994) as a useful lens for understanding how autoethnographers are able to shift between the (1) human person having an experience and (2) scholar interpreting that human experience through the lenses of their discipline. Based on these criteria, I have previously argued that Frankl's book *Man's Search for Meaning* (1946/2014) is an early example of autoethnography:

> Frankl's double consciousness is evident in this narrative; his experiences as a social scientist and sufferer allowed him to fuse the personal and the scholarly in a way that might not have been possible for other psychiatrists (who were not also prisoners) or prisoners (who were not also psychiatrists). In the Camps, Frankl recognized that his exceptional circumstance would allow him to explore psychological and philosophical assumptions about the human response to unavoidable suffering previously put forth by himself and by other scholars from the pristine comfort of the ivory tower. With this acknowledgement, he became an opportunistic researcher (see Riemer 1997), and arguably, an autoethnographer…
>
> Like publications that have previously been acknowledged as autoethnography, *Man's Search for Meaning* is the story of a single individual—in this case, a psychiatrist—in relation to the institutional, social, and political forces shaping his daily existence (see Ellis 2004). Although Frankl did not explicitly employ the autoethnographic approaches that were eventually to be identified by Heider (1975) and Hayano (1982) and further elaborated by Deborah Reed-Danahay (1997), Carolyn Ellis and Arthur Bochner (Bochner and Ellis 1996; Ellis 2004; Ellis and Bochner 2000), *Man's Search for Meaning* meets several functional characteristics of autoethnography referenced by Ellis (2004). (Esping 2010, p. 203)

As a scientist, Frankl understood that his insider status left room for skepticism toward the validity of any of the psychological or sociological inferences, interpretations, or judgments he wrote about his experiences in the camp. He made his concerns explicit in the first chapter of *Man's Search for Meaning*:

> To attempt a methodical presentation of the subject is very difficult, as psychology requires a certain scientific detachment. But does a man who makes his observations while he himself is a prisoner possess the necessary detachment? Such detachment is granted to the outsider, but he is too far removed to make any statements of real value. Only the man inside knows. His judgments may not be objective; his evaluations may be out of proportion. This is inevitable. An attempt must be made to avoid any personal bias, and that is the real difficulty of a book of this kind. At times it will be necessary to have the courage to tell of very intimate experiences. I had intended to write this book anonymously, using my prison number only. But when the manuscript was completed, I saw that as an anonymous publication it would lose half its value. (1946/2014, p. 6)

Here we see his struggle with the positivist paradigm into which he had been socialized as a scientist and the existentialist paradigm that celebrates the value of the incommutable individual perspective derived from his unique disposition, situation, and position. Radical proponent of autoethnography Carolyn Ellis asserts that while it is necessary for insider circumstances such as this to "take precautions in interpreting, generalizing, and eliminating bias here the same as we do with any data we collect" (1991, p. 30), she ultimately came to the conclusion that the benefits of insider study outweigh the risks: "Who knows better the right questions to ask than a social scientist who has lived through the experience? Who would make a better subject than a researcher consumed by wanting to figure it all out?" (Ellis 1991, pp. 30–31).

A standard method used by researchers to provide evidence for the validity of their inferences, interpretations, and judgments in an empirical piece is triangulation. This means the researcher attempts to explain data from the multiple vantage points, as in the case of triangulation by theories, methods, or investigators (Denzin 1978). Triangulation is difficult in autoethnography. However, Franklian existential psychology can help here: It asserts that transsubjectivity—which approaches truth through amalgamated positions—is best facilitated when several scholars with insider connections take advantage of their unique combinations of disposition, situation, and position rather than when a single scholar tries to move into multiple positions simultaneously (Frankl 1969/2014). The next section will offer several perceptual metaphors for defending this claim.

Perceptual Metaphors for Truth Finding

If each person's singular constellation of disposition, situation, and position makes them unique and irreplaceable, it follows that each person's perceptions of phenomena will also be unique in scope and capacity. Therefore, any discrete representation of experience—like a research article—will be incomplete, indefinite, and/or ambiguous. This may not be as problematic as it sounds. Franklian existential psychology relies on perceptional metaphors to make the case that this is not necessarily something scholars should be alarmed about.[6]

In his lectures at Harvard University, Frankl sometimes asked his students to look out of a window toward Harvard Chapel in the distance and to describe what they saw. The students would eventually discover that despite its unchanging nature, the chapel looked different to each person depending on the location of their seat in the classroom. Changing seats allowed them to see their peers' perspectives, but doing so also obscured their original view. They simply couldn't see all of "truth" at the same time. Frankl used this illustration to show that (a) there is an objective reality, and (b) no single person can ever experience or describe objective reality. He was rather dramatic in bringing home this point:

> If anyone claimed that he sees the chapel exactly as his neighbor does, I would have to say that one of them must be hallucinating. But does the difference of views in the least detract from the objectivity and reality of the chapel? Certainly it does not (1969/2014, p. 41).

Perhaps autoethnographers should put effort into fully describing what they *can* actually see, given their particular combination of disposition, situation, and position, rather than attempting to take multiple positions at the same time: Other researchers can see the chapel from other sides, so no individual scholar need attempt to do this alone. Frankl punctuated this point by describing the Harvard Shield:

[6] Other research paradigms besides existentialism rely (at least in part) on perceptual metaphors to build their cases about the "knowability" of reality. Positivism, which in many respects is the "opposite" of existentialism, is often supported by perceptual metaphors, as are some epistemologies derived from phenomenological, constructivist, and postmodern paradigms (see Carspecken 1996).

> Behind my seat you will see the shield of Harvard University, and inscribed thereon you will read *veritas*, which means truth; but as you also notice, this word is divided into three syllables which are distributed over three books, and we may well interpret this by saying that the total truth is not a universal truth, for it is not accessible to everyone. Man has rather to be satisfied with getting hold of a single aspect of the whole truth. (Frankl 1969/2014, p. 69)

Biological Cell Metaphor

Frankl used a metaphor based on cellular biology to explain that the biases inherent in each individual's unique perception of reality make a positive contribution to the collective understanding of phenomena:

> As is well known, when one-celled life forms evolve into many-celled organisms they pay the price of losing their immortality. They also sacrifice their omnipotence. They exchange all-aroundness for specificity. The highly differentiated retinal cell, for example, performs a function that no other type of cell can perform. The principle of division of labor has deprived the cell of its functional versatility, but what it has lost in the way of independent functioning is offset by its relative indispensability within the organism. (1955/1986, p. 69)

To update Frankl's quote for the context for unusually personal research: We should not necessarily demand scholars to function like unspecialized embryonic stem cells, impressively flexible, and mutually interchangeable, but should rather appreciate that the singular differentiation that has already taken place in each individual scholar is necessary for the overall health of the field (see Commission on Life Sciences 2002).

Mosaic Metaphor

Frankl also offered a metaphor from the arts, one which prefigures Laurel Richardson's (1997) notion of crystalline validity:

> In a mosaic, similarly, every particle, every individual piece of stone is incomplete, imperfect as it were, in form and color; its meaning follows only from its use in the whole. If each of the *tesseræ* contained the whole—like a miniature—each could be replaced by any of the others. A crystal

> may be perfect in its form, but for that very reason it is replaceable by any other specimen of the same crystal form; one octahedron is like any other ... For just as the uniqueness of the *tessera* is a value only in relation to the whole of the mosaic, so the uniqueness of the human personality finds its meaning entirely in its role in an integral whole. (1955/1986, p. 70)

Thus, Frankl's existential philosophy suggests that depictions of reality should be thought of as retinal cells or stones in a mosaic; they are uniquely limited, uniquely imperfect, and this is precisely why they have the potential to make valuable contributions to the collective effort to represent reality.

Taken together, these three metaphors have implications for triangulation in unusually personal research. A "true" account may be achieved progressively through the distributed efforts of several scholars who write about similar experiences as truthfully as they can from their unique positions, harnessing the gifts of disposition, and the opportunities of their situations. Generalizability will be realized gradually as more and more accounts of similar situations are published. The relative truths will function as mutual correctives that approach truth "from various sides, sometimes even in opposite directions" (Frankl 1955/1986, p. xiii). Thus, a community of scholars can encircle truth even if it cannot be fully captured.

Dimensional Ontology

Frankl's dimensional ontology also provides a clever perceptual metaphor for illustrating this idea. He summarized dimensional ontology, somewhat densely, in two laws. The meaning of the laws will be clarified by the illustrations which follow.

1. One and the same phenomenon projected out of its own dimension into different dimensions lower than its own is depicted in such a way that the individual pictures contradict one another.
2. Different phenomena projected out of their own dimension into one dimension lower than their own are depicted in such a manner that the pictures are ambiguous (1969/2014, pp. 9–10).

The meaning of these laws can be illustrated through a simulated shadow puppets game. Imagine that you are holding an empty can of soda in your hand. This soda can exists as an indivisible, three-dimensional unit.

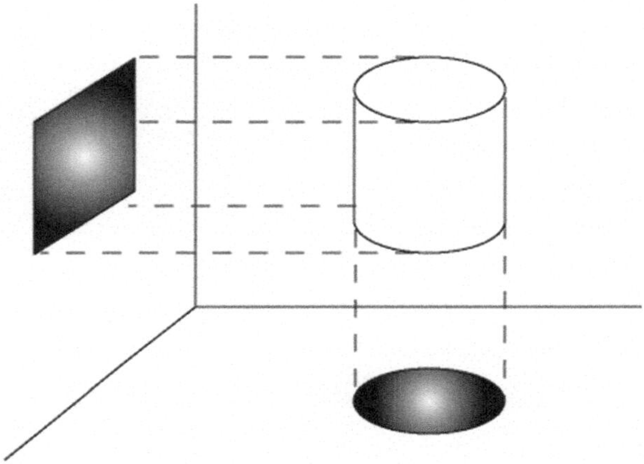

Fig. 7.1 Cylinder shadows contradict each other but are both "true" (Reprinted by permission Sidney S. Letter. From Sidney Letter (Ed.), *New Prospects for the Small Liberal Arts College*. New York: Teachers College Press. Copyright © 1968 by The Institute of Higher Education, Teachers College Press, Columbia University. All rights reserved.)

Now imagine that you were going to shine a flashlight on the soda can so you are able to see the shadow it casts on the wall behind it. Depending on how you hold the can or the flashlight, you will either see a rectangular or circular shadow cast on the wall. This is shown in Fig. 7.1.

Is the circular shadow a true depiction of the soda can? Yes. The can does have a circular component (actually two). Is the rectangular shadow a true depiction of the can? Yes. The soda can also have a rectangular component. (If the soda can were to be unfurled and flattened, its intrinsic rectangular feature would be clearer.) However, the soda can is not a circle or a rectangle. It is both of those things, but it also much more than this. It is also hollow, a dimension that the shadows do not allow us to see since the can would look the same even if it was filled with soda. Thus, the two-dimensional images projected on the wall are partial truths that contradict each other. A soda can is not a circle or a rectangle, and a circle is not a rectangle, and yet both shadows are equally "true" and limited depictions of the object. This analogy illustrates the first law of dimensional ontology.

Fig. 7.2 Morphologically dissimilar three-dimensional objects

Now imagine that you have three objects in front of you: the empty soda can, a ball, and an ice-cream cone. You now have three morphologically dissimilar three-dimensional objects, as shown in Fig. 7.2.

If you shine a flashlight from above these three objects, you would discover that the soda can, the ball, and the ice-cream cone cast identical shadows, despite their vastly different shapes, as shown in Fig. 7.3.

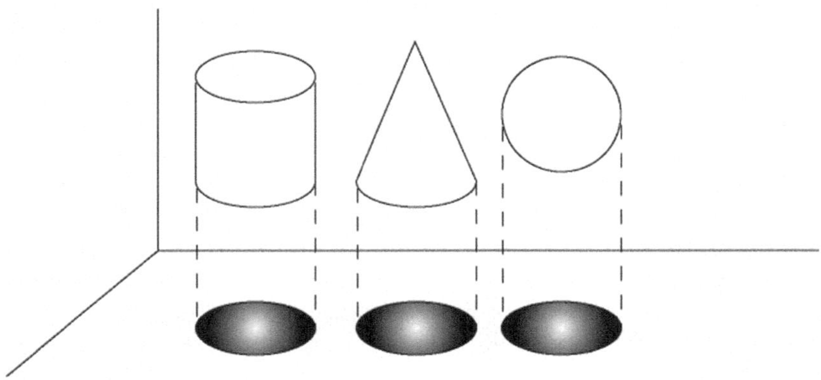

Fig. 7.3 Morphologically dissimilar objects cast identical shadows (Reprinted by permission Sidney S. Letter. From Sidney Letter (Ed.), *New Prospects for the Small Liberal Arts College*. New York: Teachers College Press. Copyright © 1968 by The Institute of Higher Education, Teachers College Press, Columbia University. All rights reserved.)

This illustrates of Frankl's second law of dimensional ontology. The three-dimensional objects are quite different in actuality, but the two-dimensional shadows created by shining light from a single perspective made it impossible to differentiate them.

These two laws, taken together, illustrate why the collective contributions of researchers from many unique positions are necessary to develop a rich, dimensionally complex picture of experience, even in the absence of objectivity. Perhaps researchers with unusually personal connections to their scholarship should not attempt to defend themselves against accusations of bias, but should rather "show that there's something to be gained by saturating [their] observations with [their] own subjectivity" and to "confront the issue of bias head-on in their own writing" (Ellis 2004, p. 89). This suggestion echoes Frankl's paraphrase of Kierkegaard, that individuals should embrace their bias in the service of truth:

> As long as we do not have access to absolute truth, we must be content that our relative truths correct one another, and that we find the courage to be biased. In the many-voiced orchestra… we not only have the right, but the duty to be biased as long as we are conscious of it. (2000, p. 126)

Conclusions

Existentialism emphasizes the particular over the general, so this makes it a problematic paradigm for supporting research. However, an existential framework can be useful for defending scholarship practices that are already controversial, like autoethnography. This chapter explored what this defense might look like. We end with a bulleted review of some major ideas and a set of existential questions for readers.

Review of Existential Epistemology

- All forms of existentialism value human uniqueness. Frankl claimed that each person's uniqueness results from the combination of three things: disposition (talents and limitations), situation (circumstances and environment), and positions (chosen attitudes and/or actions taken toward disposition and situation).
- Since all forms of existentialism emphasize the particular over the general, generalizing from a single study is not a priority.
- Du Bois' "double consciousness" (1887, 1903/1994) is a useful lens for understanding how insider researchers may shift between

their identities as a person who is living an experience and a scholar who is interpreting that experience.

- Perceptual metaphors based on a chapel, the Harvard shield, a cell, and a stone in a mosaic can be used to defend the value of transsubjectivity.
- Transsubjectivity contributes to generalization and by extension, validity.
- The two laws of dimensional ontology work together to illustrate why the collective contributions of researchers from many unique positions are needed to discover "truth" about phenomena. This can happen even in the absence of objectivity.

Existential Questions for Readers

1. Take a minute to think about one of your most meaningful scholarly projects. In what ways are your disposition and situation relevant to this project, if at all? What positions did you take/are you taking with regard to this disposition and situation? Are there other positions you could take? If the project is incomplete, are there better ways to utilize your disposition and situation to complete this project? Is there any way in which an analysis of your disposition, situation, and position(s) can illuminate why you have identified this project as being "meaningful" for you?
2. Are there new research areas you could explore that would take advantage of any opportunities you have because of your disposition and situation?
3. Consider Frankl's dimensional ontology and the other metaphors for bias presented in this chapter. Are there any ways in which these are useful for defending aspects of your scholarship? Would these pose any ethical or epistemological challenges to your scholarship?
4. Are there any areas of your life that are worth exploring through autoethnography? Would this be viewed as a defensible form of scholarship in your discipline? (e.g., Could it keep you from getting tenure? Becoming full professor? Could it help you achieve these professional goals?)

References

Bochner, A. P., & Ellis, C. (1996). Talking over ethnography. In C. Ellis & A. P. Bochner (Eds.), *Composing ethnography: Alternative forms of qualitative writing* (pp. 13–45). Walnut Creek, CA: AltaMira.

Carspecken, P. F. (1996). *Critical ethnography in educational research: A theoretical and practical guide*. New York: Routledge.

Commission on Life Sciences. (2002). *Stem cells and the future of regenerative medicine*. Washington, DC: National Academy Press.

Denzin, N. K. (1978). *Sociological methods*. New York: McGraw-Hill.

Denzin, N. K., & Lincoln, Y. S. (Eds.). (2003). *The landscape of qualitative research: Theories and issues* (2nd ed.). Thousand Oaks, CA: Sage.

Du Bois, W. E. B. (1887, August). Strivings of the Negro people. *The Atlantic*, p. 197.

Du Bois, W. E. B. (1903/1994). *The souls of black folk*. New York: Dover.

Duckworth, A. L., Peterson, C., Matthews, M. D., & Kelly, D. R. (2007). Grit: Perseverance and passion for long-term goals. *Journal of Personality and Social Psychology, 92*(6), 1087–1101.

Ellis, C. (1991). Sociological introspection and emotional experience. *Symbolic Interaction, 14*, 23–50.

Ellis, C. (2004). *The ethnographic I: A methodological novel about autoethnography*. Walnut Creek, CA: AltaMira.

Ellis, C., & Bochner, A. P. (Eds.). (1996). *Composing ethnography: Alternative forms of ethnographic writing*. Walnut Creek, CA: AltaMira.

Ellis, C., & Bochner, A. P. (2000). Autoethnography, personal narrative, reflexivity. In N. K. Denzin & Y. S. Lincoln (Eds.), *Handbook of qualitative research* (2nd ed., pp. 733–768). Thousand Oaks, CA: Sage.

Esping, A. (2010). Autoethnography and existentialism: The conceptual contributions of Viktor Frankl. *Journal of Phenomenological Psychology, 41*(2), 201–215.

Esping, A. (2011). Autoethnography as logotherapy: An existential analysis of meaningful social science inquiry. *Journal of Border Educational Research, 9*(1), 59–68.

Fox, K. V. (1996). A subversive reading of child sexual abuse. In C. Ellis & A. Bochner (Eds.), *Composing ethnography: Alternative forms of ethnographic writing* (pp. 330–356). Walnut Creek, CA: AltaMira.

Frankl, V. E. (1946/2014). *Man's search for meaning*. Boston: Beacon Press.

Frankl, V. E. (1955/1986). *The doctor and the soul*. New York: Vintage Books.

Frankl, V. E. (1969/2014). *The will to meaning: Foundations and applications of logotherapy*. New York: Meridian.

Frankl, V. E. (2000). *Recollections: An autobiography* (J. Fabry & J. Fabry, Trans.). Cambridge: Basic Books.

Hayano, D. M. (1982). *Poker faces.* Berkeley: University of California Press.

Heider, K. (1975). What do people do? Dani auto-ethnography. *Journal of Anthropological Research, 31,* 3–17.

Mead, M. (1928/2001). *Coming of age in Samoa: A psychological study of primitive youth for Western civilization.* New York: William Morrow.

Rambo Ronai, C. (1996). My mother is mentally retarded. In C. Ellis & A. Bochner (Eds.), *Composing ethnography: Alternative forms of ethnographic writing* (pp. 109–131). Walnut Creek, CA: AltaMira.

Reed-Danahay, D. E. (Ed.). (1997). *Auto/ethnography: Rewriting the self and the social.* New York: Berg.

Richardson, L. (1997). *Fields of play: Constructing an academic life.* New Brunswick, NJ: Rutgers University Press.

Ridley, M. (2003). *Nature via nurture: Genes, experience, and what makes us human.* New York: HarperCollins.

Riemer, J. W. (1977). Varieties of opportunistic research. *Urban Life, 5,* 467–477.

Sanborn, P. F. (1968). *Existentialism.* New York: Pegasus.

Tillmann-Healy, L. (1996). A secret life in a culture of thinness: Reflections on body, food and bulimia. In C. Ellis & A. Bochner (Eds.), *Composing ethnography: Alternative forms of ethnographic writing* (pp. 76–108). Walnut Creek, CA: AltaMira.

CHAPTER 8

Ethical Dilemmas in Unusually Personal Research

Jesse	*You don't know what it's like to be trans.*
Amber	*No.*
Jesse	*You don't know. Do you know what it's like to be afraid?*
Amber	*Yes.*
Jesse	*Do you know what it's like to feel alone?*
Amber	*Yes.*
Jesse	*Do you know what it's like to feel misunderstood?*
Amber	*Yes.*
Jesse	*Do you know what it's like to feel strange and different from everybody else?*
Amber	*[big pause] [sigh], Yes, but I hesitate to—to—*
Jesse	*Don't compare. Just—*
Amber	*Yeah. Sure.*
Jesse	*Yeah. Okay. Let's go from there.*
Amber	*Okay.*
Jesse	*You may never know what this feels like in your body.*
Amber	*Um-hum.*
Jesse	*But I would trust you to talk about transgenderism to people.*
Amber	*Really? I wouldn't trust me.*
Jesse	*Maybe not from a stage, but from knowing me I would trust you more than I would trust someone who's never been around a trans person.*
Amber	*Okay.*
Jesse	*Okay? I trust you to take my words and make meaning out of them in your book.*
Amber	*Hmm. Actually that's a good point. You are trusting me.*

—Jesse, Gender Identity Scholar and Activist, 2017

A. Esping, *Epistemology, Ethics, and Meaning in Unusually Personal Scholarship*, https://doi.org/10.1007/978-3-319-73718-8_8

This is an excerpt from my most recent interview with the transgender scholar, Jesse. We were talking about whether someone who has not "been there" can truly understand someone else's experience. As a qualitative researcher, obviously I hope that I can get inside other people's experiences and then represent those experiences authentically in print. However, any casual perusal of validity (also called "trustworthiness") literature in the social sciences makes it clear how arrestingly complicated and controversial any attempt at this is. Mainstream researchers, who are for the most part outsiders with respect to the phenomena they study, must closely examine the philosophical underpinnings of their scholarship with regard to ontology (what is/what is real?), epistemology (how do I come to know what is real?), axiology (what role do values play in research?), and methodology (what choices should I make with regard to my research approach?). Autoethnographers and conventional researchers with unusually personal connections to their areas of study must be especially sensitive to these concerns. They must also contend with ethical dilemmas arising from their unique relationships to their areas of inquiry. The present chapter will use interview data from the two social scientist Case Study participants, Gillian and Jesse, and the physicist, Ron, to investigate some of the relevant issues. Peggy's data are not included here because her bioethics scholarship is not usually empirical in nature.

The "Real Thing"

In 1580, the French Renaissance philosopher Michel de Montaigne wrote this:

> A man must have experienced all the illnesses he hopes to cure and all the accidents and circumstances he is to diagnose…Such a man I would trust. For the rest guide us like the person who paints seas, rocks and harbors while sitting at his table and sails his model of a ship in perfect safety. Throw him into the real thing, and he does not know where to begin. (Montaigne 1580/2003)

One characteristic that differentiates my Case Study participants from most other researchers in their fields is that they have experienced "the real thing." Like Frankl, they are scholars with street cred.

I have maintained throughout this book that Frankl's ability to combine his academic and personal perspectives on human suffering served important epistemological purposes for the creation of *Man's Search for Meaning* (1946/2014). Psychiatrists and prisoners understand the horrors of the concentration camp experience in different ways. Since Frankl could draw on both funds of knowledge (see Gonzáles et al. 2005), he could create and communicate a more dimensional representation of the experience than could a psychiatrist who was not also a prisoner, or a prisoner who was not also a psychiatrist. To borrow perceptual metaphors from Chapter 7, he was able to perceive contrapositive sides of the Harvard Chapel concurrently. Or perhaps, just perhaps, he wasn't describing shadows on a wall, but was uniquely able to see the soda can, the cone, and the ball in situ. In prior chapters, I have also interpreted this in terms of his double consciousness (see Du Bois 1887, 1903/1994; Reed-Danahay 1997) and identity intersectionality (Crenshaw 1989). But what do the Case Study participants think about this? Do they believe insiders with research training have epistemological advantages?

Gillian, The Bereaved Parent

As a social scientist who is also a sufferer, Gillian felt she was in a unique position to make contributions to her field of study. The wisdom and insight gleaned from her personal experiences were a strength from which she drew when writing and speaking in professional contexts. She placed high importance on the opportunity to integrate her personal reflections into academic papers, and she viewed her insider perspective as one of the strengths of her writing. Her dissertation Chair encouraged the use of first person in her papers, and the audience reviews she showed me of her presentation at an Association of Death Education and Counseling (ADEC) conference lauded her personal approach. However, many professors discourage or even forbid the use of "I" in scholarly work. When Gillian took classes from these professors, she felt as if some valuable resources were walled off. For example, in a child development class, she was required to write ten papers relating her dissertation topic to child development. Gillian wanted to use these assignments to explore grief and loss as she had witnessed it "through the eyes" of her daughter. However, because she was not permitted to use the first-person voice, she had to "completely change" her approach. It was difficult for her to be motivated to do this work, and she found it "hard" not be able to put her own "twist on things" and include her "own insight."

I asked Gillian what she thought of Montaigne's quote about sailing a model ship. Were the inferences, interpretations, and judgments she came to as part of her empirical scholarship more trustworthy than those of competent, well-trained outsiders? Gillian has always maintained that her dissertation Chair, a bereavement researcher who had never lost a child, "gets it." This was in part not only because of her Chair's professional training, but also because this expert had lost a relative to suicide. There were "overlaps" in these two tragedies. However, Gillian also believed that with the right attitude and methodologies she could get into her participants' understanding in her present work as an educational technology researcher. This work is very mainstream and not at all dependent on her own insider experience:

> All the interventions we do, whatever population we are working with, we work from the bottom up, always. I'm sure you probably do that because you're a qualitative researcher too. Like if we're using educational technology for at risk teens, then the at-risk teens are the ones that are helping us use educational technology. We're not the experts up here trying to tell them what they need to do. They need to tell us, and we need to build from the bottom up. So that's why when I look at this [Montaigne quote], that's how I'm looking at it. It's the people that are experiencing it, that's where we need to learn. They're the ones with the voices. They're the ones that I trust. It's not going to be the person that's up here [*indicates a space above us*], painting the picture thinking they understand it.

From this I take it that she believes an insider understanding helpful, but not necessary. That said, Gillian also believed that her insider understanding of parental bereavement could be an asset on a bereavement research team. Interview participants might be more willing to open up to someone who has had similar experiences, resulting in richer, more authentic, data:

> How much better to have an insider! Because if I wanted to do research with bereaved parents, me just sitting down and saying, "I lost a child too. I'm a bereaved parent. I lost a child too. Let's talk." That person is probably more likely to be more open and be able to say things that they couldn't say—Because I know that feeling, too, of trying to explain something to somebody and I'm like, "They don't get it because they just don't

> understand." You know, they don't get it...It's powerful...I could be very valuable on a team just because of what I could bring in, in terms of talking to someone.

But could her insider status influence the data in less productive ways because of her preexisting beliefs and values? Recall that in Chapter 2 she repeatedly used the metaphor of getting her "voice heard" through her scholarship. Might her voice overpower the voices of her research participants? Was her child development professor correct in asking her to try to step outside of her personal experience when writing about her dissertation topic? Gillian had confidence in her social science training and felt the best approach to dealing with her bias was to own it. Bias is not all bad. Sometimes those hard-wrought personal understandings can fill in gaps in the data. And besides, she claimed, no one is really objective anyway:

> Even if we try to pretend we're objective, we're not. Nobody is...We all come in with biases, and I don't think that's necessarily a bad thing. I think it's more of a disclaimer, "This is where I'm coming from. Take it or leave it." [*laughing*] But I think it can be a very powerful thing, too. I don't think anybody wants somebody coming in that hasn't—Because you can try to explain it in so many words what it's like to lose a child, but unless you've experienced it, it's like you can't. There aren't any words to do it, I think.

Jesse, The Transgender Scholar

Long before he thought of gathering statistical data, Jesse had already explored the two-sex/two-gender paradigm intimately from the inside. In his first interview during graduate school, Jesse explained that this visceral experience offered both epistemological and motivational advantages:

> I think I have an ability to *understand* that perhaps...people who've never been conflicted about their gender might not have...Like in the intersexed thing. I don't know what it's like to have ten genital surgeries by the age of 10...I can only pretend to know...But I know what it's like to get *shit* from society because you don't fit this cookie cutter idea of what your sex should be. I know that personally. I know it beyond an academic,

intellectual [level]...Maybe I'll dig a little deeper...Maybe I'll go an extra mile. Maybe I'll have an insight that somebody else might not be able to have.

In the years following his first interview, Jesse gave many presentations on the topic of sex and gender identity. In these talks, he offered theoretical perspectives on these constructs, provided medical information about intersexuality, transsexuality, and transgenderism, and shared his own story of growing up as a transgender person. The positive public response to these talks confirmed the value he placed on his insider understanding. In his final year of graduate school, Jesse explained:

I have a perspective that a typically gendered person does not have. And I view that perspective as an advantage. There are things that I see so *clearly*, and when I say them to people, [they say] "*Wow*. Whoa." And to me, it's just so clear. But it's clear because of my experience. Because of who I am. And I think that's a real plus.

In order to further explore the advantages of an insider understanding to a professional researcher, I asked Jesse if a typically gendered person like myself could ever deeply understand the experiences of atypically gendered people. He responded this way:

Yes. I just don't know that you could get there on your own. I've pretty much gotten there on my own. I think you would have to really seek it out and find it. But I've gotten it just from *life*. I'm not sure you could get it just from life. I think you'd have to say "I want to understand this. I'm gonna have to go after it".

This seems to echo Gillian's perspective that insider status is helpful, but not necessary for approaching trustworthy empirical understandings. Approximately 10 years after he graduated with his Ph.D., I showed Jesse Montaigne's quote about the model ship. What did he think about the value of an insider perspective now? First, he found the quote too melodramatic:

I get what he's saying, but I'm also seeing a little bit of martyrdom in this. We *love* the story—The hero's journey. We *love* the story of the person who has had just all this shit happen to him and then rises from the flames like the Phoenix. We *love* that shit. Look at our movies! Can you imagine

> a movie where someone was just happy, and had a good time, and enjoyed life? We'd be bored to death! Right? So what do we do? We say, "Oh, I have to have something to complain about too." And we sit around and complain, right? And, you know, I do this too, but we sit around and complain and we wear it as a badge of honor that "I've suffered! And this has been my pain!" What if life were supposed to feel good? What if life were supposed to be fun? Well only if you suffer for it and earn it! You know?

At this point, Jesse led me through the dialogue I used for this chapter's epigraph. He then told me a story about a presentation he gave at a conference focusing on LGBT+ issues. Early in his career, Jesse believed that as a transgender person, he could count on support from other members of the LGBT+ community, such as transsexuals, intersexed people, gay men, and lesbians:

> And at this point I was still kind of naïve in that, "We're all under this umbrella together, and we all have each other's back, and isn't it great!" That was back before I realized that there are a lot of gay people who have problems with trans people, and transsexuals have problems with me, and all of that stuff. But anyway, there's this guy there. And I said, "Oh, are you presenting?" "Yes." I said, "What are you presenting on?" He said something to do with intersexuality. He was an intersexed gentleman. And I said, "Oh, that's fantastic! [And he asked] "What are you talking about?"…I said, "Well, I talk about the fallacies of the dichotomous way of looking at sex and gender, that's evidenced by transgender people and intersexed people and I think humanity would be better if we could loosen that up." [He said] "Huh." That's about all he said…and then I went to his talk…And halfway through his talk…he looked directly at me. And he went, "And transgender people, stop using intersexuality as an excuse for being transgender! No one but an intersexed person should be telling an intersexed story!" And then he looked away and kept talking…I thought, "hmm. That's interesting."…And I thought about that for several days. I thought, "Wow. Maybe I should stop talking about intersexuality." And then another part of me, after a few days of this, said, "Dude, if you want to see *me* as the enemy, knock yourself out. Because I am having people coming to me saying, "I had *no idea* intersexuality existed." I am doing something worthwhile here, and if you want to see me as the enemy, go ahead. I'm not intersexed, but I can tell people about the condition of intersexuality and what we as a society and the medical community has done historically to intersexed people. I can tell that, and I can tell that in a powerful way that makes people question their beliefs about sex and

gender without being an intersexed person. Now I think being transgender maybe helped me get into that. But I'm not intersexed, but I can still talk about the experience. So no, I'd don't agree that "A man must have experienced all the illnesses he hopes to cure, and all the accidents and circumstances he hopes to diagnose." I think it's an overstatement. That's what I would say.

Ethical Dilemma: Having a "Mission" and Changing Your Mind

Viktor Frankl had already developed the core tenets of logotherapy before entering the concentration camps. Therefore, his conclusion in *Man's Search for Meaning* (1946/2014) that mental health depends on finding meaning in suffering represents an affirmation and confirmation of his preexisting beliefs, rather than a new discovery grounded in data. I have no ethical concerns about this since Frankl did not claim to be conducting research for that book. But what if he *had* been doing research? The two social scientists from the Part I Case Studies, Gillian and Jesse, saw graduate school as part of their "mission" to change other people's minds. Jesse wanted to make the case in his dissertation that the two-sex/two-gender paradigm is not sufficient for describing human experience. Gillian wanted to use her scholarship to convince people that what they have probably heard about bereavement "is just wrong." This raises important questions about their ability to change their *own* minds when confronted with data that do not match their preexisting agenda. Can a scholar have a self-described "mission" to change people's minds and also conduct trustworthy research in that area?

Gillian's Openness to Changing Her Mind

Before Gillian entered graduate school, she had already formed the opinion that "what people tell you" about bereavement "is just—just wrong." She also felt confident that "there had to be something out there that could assist bereaved parents to get through the loss of a child...with...less struggle than I had." Given this strong opinion and sense of purpose, I was curious to see how her ideas would evolve as a function of her interaction with theories, data, and professional experts during graduate school. Her personal experience with bereavement and her passionate dedication to the cause of helping others like herself had implications for her willingness to change her mind when confronted with ideas and data that did not match her own preexisting beliefs.

Gillian's data reveal that she was open to changing her mind. When she started graduate school, she was convinced that bereaved parents needed "tangible" help in the form of programs. Exposure to the bereavement literature and several conversations with her dissertation Chair convinced her to shift her focus away from programs and toward the study of internal resources that bereaved parents can harness to find meaning in their loss. Instrumental to this change was research she did for a class paper during her first semester of graduate school; the literature she read convinced her that "programs to help bereaved parents do little."

When I interviewed Gillian during her second year of graduate school, she admitted that it was "hard to detach" her personal experience when she was researching and writing. This was one reason she felt it important to disclose her personal experience in publications:

> In scholarly papers I make sure to write, you know, who I am…I *am* a bereaved parent…I am an upcoming expert, I do feel, in my field, but I'm also a bereaved parent. So the things that you will read…it's my own experience plus what I have…interpreted and read. So I always make sure to say that up front.

We see here how Gillian carefully negotiated the roles of bereaved parent and "upcoming expert" in parental bereavement. She did not want her insider understanding to blind her to data that were inconsistent with her own preconceived ideas, but she also felt that her preconceived ideas had value:

> A lot of people say I cannot be objective because I'm so absorbed in it… [and] because I've already created my idea of how things are to be… But *my* thought on that is that's my strength…I *do* know what I'm talking about from my own personal [experience]… as long as you kind of *own* that part and say, "As a researcher I am also a bereaved parent, and… this is how it's influenced my work." I always try to put that in there just because…it kind of takes that…objective part way. Because I'm owning it. I'm owning that I'm a bereaved parent, and I'm owning that that's gonna obviously reflect how I write and the things that I see are important and the things…that kind of stand out to me that may not stand out to somebody else.

When I asked Gillian how she dealt with data that did not match her own experience, she gave several examples. In her first interview, she compared her own aversion to the construct of "moving on" as part of the bereavement process with a few studies showing that some parents are "able to detach from their child completely and move on…It's not the norm, but it does happen." In her second interview during graduate school, she expressed "surprise" and sometimes "frustration" at some of the things the husbands said about their wives in the interviews she analyzed for her thesis:

> [The] men are very much "I've gone through the stages of grief. She hasn't. She's still stuck in denial." And it's like "No no!" You just want to reach in there and be like, "There are no stages of grief" and "We all grieve differently" and "She's not stuck. This is where she is." Because I feel where she is. I know *exactly* where she is.

During data analysis, for her master's thesis became "more aware" of the fact that "others don't think like me." As a social scientist, she also found it interesting that not every parent tried to find meaning in the loss of a child. As a bereaved parent who personally found tremendous comfort in the search for meaning, she found the nihilistic attitude puzzling. On more than one occasion, she wanted to reach out to a parent who expressed these sentiments in a transcript and urge them to try to find meaning. Instead, she reported what she found and moved on.

Gillian described her paradigmatic orientation toward research as "constructivist" which for her meant, "we construct our reality. That we construct…our stories." She also believed human beings are "wired to make sense of things in stories." This constructivist theoretical orientation leaves open the possibility of multiple interpretations of data; she was not attempting to be a positivist. This approach would be clear to the consumers of her research because of the way she described her methods. Gillian's self-awareness with regard to how her life experience impacted her beliefs, her openness to changing her mind when she encountered surprising data, and her conviction that it was important to disclose her identity as a bereaved parent builds confidence that her bereavement research was as trustworthy as that of any qualified dispassionate "outsider."

Jesse's Openness to Changing His Mind

Before applying to graduate school, Jesse had already decided that the two-sex/two-gender paradigm was "erroneous." He hoped that his program would give him the training and opportunity to look for solid empirical evidence to support this claim. This self-described "mission" had implications for the validity of his research. Jesse was keenly aware of these implications and had given them quite a bit of thought before I asked him about them. Indeed, he posed several rhetorical questions about this during our first graduate school interview. These questions were just exploratory. He did not offer answers:

> I think there's *risk* in exploring yourself…If I did a study and uncovered something *horrible* about transgender people, would I publish it? I mean if I found evidence that it's a *choice* would I publish that?…If I found evidence that it *is* a mental illness, what would I do with that?…Would I handle that differently than if I was studying something I didn't have a personal stake in?

When Jesse was nearing his Ph.D. graduation, I invited him to label the philosophical paradigm that had been supporting his approach to research. He replied that he was a "practicing postpositivist who respects the qualitative side of things." When asked to define postpositivism, he answered in part, "maybe we can't really be objective, but we're going to try." He preferred using statistical, rather than qualitative, analyses in his own work because quantitative tools "complement the way I think." Jesse did not equate these attempts at objectivity with being detached. Indeed, he described himself as a very "passionate" researcher. Moreover, he did not believe that passion was incompatible with honest scientific inquiry. To illustrate his position, Jesse told me a humorous story about a class presentation he gave during his second semester of graduate school:

> My presentation was questioning the medical management of intersexuality. And that's the first presentation I gave in graduate school. And it set the stage for how the rest of my life was going to be in grad school because everybody else was talking about things like classroom management and I was talking about ambiguous genitalia. And…I was the first presenter *[laughing]*…I hit 'em with all of this stuff. And I was pretty passionate. And the feedback that I got from the professor afterwards—this

> was not…official feedback—This was just kind of a friendly, "Hey, for the future this is something you probably ought to know." But the professor said, "Well you'll learn as you mature in this [field] to provide a more balanced presentation and to not be so overtly [passionate]"…And at the time I thought, "What the hell's wrong with passion?" What? Huh? *[little laugh]*. But I kind of…filed it away…Then I took a qualitative research class and I actually wrote a reflection about this…Why *should* I temper my passion? And I *have*…some pretty strong opinions. And I'm going to try to find empirical evidence to support my opinions. And that's no different than any other scientist. That's no different than somebody studying bacteria. You know, they *have* a theory that they feel pretty strongly about or they wouldn't go to the time and expense and trouble to test it. And of *course* they're going to run tests…that they believe are going to support their theories. And when it doesn't get supported you report that…Why should I tone down my rhetoric just to *appear* more objective? I mean, is anyone really objective? I don't think so. The guy studying bacteria is not objective. He's trying to find evidence for his theories.

In response to this story, I challenged Jesse with a question similar to the ones he had posited in his first interview three years earlier: What would he do if he found evidence in his research that there were only two genders? Jesse replied:

> Well that has to do with integrity…and being ethical…If that happens then that's what I gotta report. And that's what I gotta start writing about. And then I gotta start writing about what that means for people like me.

Like Gillian, Jesse believed that it was impossible for any researcher to be completely objective, but perhaps unlike Gillian he felt an ethical obligation to try. His dissertation proposal was approximately 100 pages long, and the completed dissertation was nearly 200 pages—substantially longer than is typical for a quantitative study in his field. Taking into account his vulnerability as a transgender researcher, he felt it was important to be especially thorough and provide logical critiques of the methodology and conclusions of previous relevant studies presented in his literature review. Jesse hoped this careful attention to the work of other experts would help establish his professional credibility. As he put it, "It wasn't just a hundred pages of me saying, 'I think this.'"

Ethical Dilemma: To Disclose or Not?

Given these epistemological challenges, it is reasonable to assume that some researchers will never disclose the unusually personal motivations for their scholarship. Perhaps they have received messages from professors, dissertation committees, or peers that revealing personal motivations will make them appear too biased. Perhaps in reality they *are* too biased, but since they aren't sharing their background, how would we know? Maybe these scholars worry that disclosing any unusually personal connections to their research agendas will have an adverse impact on their tenure decisions or their acceptance as serious scholars worthy of publication in high-impact journals, even if they've done everything "right" according to the standards for research in their particular discipline. In academia, as in so much of the rest of life, appearance sometimes matters more than substance. But a veneer of emotional indifference and merely intellectual curiosity does not change the deeper reality.

Secrecy can be thought of as a reasonable response to potentially uninformed attacks on a researcher's credibility. Therefore, important stakeholders will never truly know the impetus for some research in their field, even though the directions of their fields may be influenced by this work. Recall that theoretical physicist Ronald Mallet did not disclose his motivation to his thesis Chair during graduate school and waited until after tenure and promotion to full professor before showing his father's picture during a conference presentation attended by leaders in his field. He called this "coming out of the time travel closet." Before reaching the important milestones of tenure and promotion, he was concerned that his special circumstances might have earned him a reputation as a "nut" or a "crackpot." But once he had established a solid reputation in the field, this was no longer a concern. In our interview, he stated that, having gotten that far in his career, his personal story simply made him more interesting to his colleagues and had no bearing on their critiques of his work. In physics, the science speaks for itself:

> What my colleagues respect is that part of it. They respect the fact that I spent all these years to become a physicist. And I've done papers on more than just time travel. I've done papers that have been published on black holes, on cosmology, the big bang theory, quantum physics…These are the papers that were behind what lead me to get my tenure. So my colleagues

respect that. Because you might say, I'm part of the club. So they respect me for that. So their critiques come from a place of respect...And we're all in this calling together, so we appreciate what goes into that calling. Because we *know* the silent hours of grueling over laboratory apparatus and breaking our head against the equations. We all know that, and we all went through the same thing to get that. Okay? So we respect that. What we argue about is when we get the results. That's the important part. That's why we have these refereed, you know, the peer review thing. But with my colleagues [my personal story] isn't what leads to it. It's whether or not what I've done is good physics.

Given how carefully he timed his "coming out," I asked Ron what advice he would give to a young physicist with an unusual motivation for his research agenda. Would he advise this young student to disclose his controversial goals? Here is what he said:

I would say find a faculty member that's willing to work on that idea, [but] I'm skeptical that you will. Because they want to work on *their* ideas. That's fine. But what I would suggest is that you look what faculty have to offer that's close to what it is that you're doing. Because you're not going to get your degree if no one wants to take you on for your idea...I wouldn't say give up your idea...If you really believe in your idea, what you should do is find a faculty member who is working close to that area. And then you can develop your idea *after* you've gotten your degree. You see? That's the way I would phrase it. Because now I'm using my own experience, because that's what happened. And it worked for me. So I was able to have my cake and eat it too. I found someone whose work was close enough to what I was wanting to do. And I could work on that, and at the same time learn more about what it is that I wanted to do. I could get my degree, and then I could go off and, you know, work on that.

Unlike Ron, health behavior researcher Gillian disclosed her intentionality immediately upon entering graduate school. No one ever accused her of having "blind spots," or expressed concern about the credibility of the social science work she was doing. She did, however, feel discomfort at the vulnerability her openness created. Here is how she explained it approximately ten years after she graduated:

I always got a lot of *wonderful* support from the research community... It was just very hard to do. It was hard to present. It was just hard to talk about. It still is....It's hard to feel very professional when you break down

> a lot. And it's also, too, it's like you're letting strangers know these very personal things sometimes, and it makes you feel vulnerable. And I don't like that aspect. People sensing I'm vulnerable. Especially if you want to be a professional, appear to be professional. Like this sense that you're being vulnerable. And some people can do it very gracefully. I'm a *mess*. I just break down. I just cry. I cry when I'm happy, I cry when I'm sad, I cry when I'm not even thinking about things! [*laughing*] So yeah, it makes it much harder.

Despite the vulnerability, Gillian would advise graduate students to disclose their unusually personal motivations. When I asked her if they should, here is how she responded:

> Oh absolutely! Absolutely…We have professors and researchers and people come in to talk to high school students a lot at the [education technology] lab. Because we have a lot high school interns…And the things that are the most impactful to *them* are the stories of why they got into research, no matter what it is. Whether they're a gynecologist or obstetrician or a medical doctor. Whatever they're doing, it's the personal story of how they got into it and why that is the most powerful and the most meaningful when you listen to them talk. And the students take it away, too. Their captivated, their caught. So I think without the passion or the drive, it's kind of—That's where the meaning *is*. 'Cause you're wanting to add something. It becomes very personal.

Transgender social scientist Jesse was closeted for the first part of graduate school, but he used his scholarship as part of his coming-out process. He found his graduate school colleagues very affirming throughout and at times certain faculty members less so. In his first faculty position, he experienced some pretty overt discrimination. His next position was very accepting. When I asked him if he would advise a young transgender scholar to come out if they were studying transgender issues, he responded this way:

> That's gotta be their decision. I'd probably talk to them about pros and cons, and process that with them. You know, if you don't, and you get outed, what does that look like?…Oh you know, "Oh, well, you had an agenda." I would never say, "Well you need to come out." I would never say that to someone.

When I asked him what he meant by "pros and cons," he explained:

> Well, there's something about putting your cards on the table…"Here's my biases. Here they are. I can't change this…Now that we've said that, let's go on." So there's value in that. But, if you come out and you're not ready, you just come out because you think you're supposed to, then you may not be prepared when your colleagues are laughing at you in the hall, or when the students point and whisper behind your back that you know, "There this weirdo is." So, maybe they're not out to their family, and then their family finds out some other way. It's complicated stuff, and all that has to be considered.

This response was very sensitive to the needs of the transgender student. But I probed further to see what Jesse would say about the needs of the field. What concerns, if any, would he have working with this person in the capacity of research advisor?

> Well, I think it depends on the situation. If it's an angry person, that would be a concern to me. If someone were totally closeted and just petrified of being found out, that could be concerning. Because you could get accused—Great example. Have you ever heard the transcript of Reagan's press secretary the first time AIDS was mentioned in a question/answer? There was a [reporter]…He said, "has the president heard about this Acquired Immune Deficiency Syndrome that's hitting gay men? And everybody laughed. And the press secretary, whoever he was, said something like, "Pfft. Well I don't have [AIDS]! Do you? Do you have [AIDS]?"And this went on for months. And the reporter was like, "Hey, this is a serious thing. You know, 80% of the people who had it have died", or whatever the numbers were. And then, you know, there's other clips where he kept bringing it up. And it got to where he'd bring it up, and the [press secretary] would be like, "Ugh. I don't get paid enough for this."…Now this went on for years, and like hundreds of thousands of gay men died. But just this reporter asking the question, the immediate response was, "Well are you gay? Now that was a long time ago, but it makes the point I'm trying to make. Just you writing about this, somebody who wants to attack your work, could say, "well you must be one of these weirdos." And if you're *so afraid* of being found out, are you gonna be able to handle that? So that's a con. If you're going to do this work, you're going to come under fire at some point. Can you handle it? [As a defense], be good at what you do. If you're good at what you do, especially if you're doing

something that's valued, people will accept a lot. It's harder to be denied tenure if you're good at what you do.

We can see from these varied responses that the decisions of whether, and when, to disclose unusually personal connections to research is an important issue that graduate students and faculty pay close attention to. Gillian disclosed right away, the major ill-effect being a heightened sense of vulnerability. Jesse disclosed in the midst of graduate school, and "putting his cards on the table" felt like an ethical and healthful option in his case. Ron waited until he reached the safe position of tenured full professor. With an *n* of 3, and three different responses, it is difficult to reach any generalizable conclusions with regard to disclosing personal connections to research. However, it is clear that when researchers keep personal connections secret, colleagues and mentors cannot intervene when extra emotional, ethical, or epistemological support is warranted. Perhaps this should be an ongoing conversation in research courses and mentoring and advising relationships.

Conclusions

I have found various incarnations of this quote all over the Internet: "From the inside it's impossible to explain. From the outside it's impossible to understand." People invoke this aphorism to explain everything from eating disorders and depression to being part of a sorority. Apparently it is a popular quote to print on sorority T-shirts. Before I began writing this chapter, I wondered if it should be could be on some researchers' T-shirts, too. Now I'm not so sure.Gillian and Jesse believe that they have some epistemological advantages because they are insiders, but they do not seem to think that insiders are the only ones who can understand and represent aspects of their experiences. They trust mainstream inquiry methodologies to get other researchers close to their hard-wrought understandings. In this way, their views are at odds with Frankl's statement about writing about his imprisonment, "Only the man inside knows" (Frankl 1946/2014, p. 6).

Gillian and Jesse are also quite aware that their close connections to their research topics have resulted in bias. Neither is apologetic. Rather, they agree that the best thing for a scholar to do is to articulate biases boldly and then let readers or listeners judge their work in its merits. The merits of Gillian's constructivist-based work will be assessed differently than the merits of research conducted by the postpositivist Jesse. Gillian's interview data also provide evidence that she was willing to change her mind when she read things that didn't jibe with her preexisting beliefs about parental bereavement. Jesse didn't provide specific examples of when he has changed his mind, but his postpositivist research paradigm, his emphasis on "integrity," and his 200-page quantitative dissertation suggest that he is meticulous about defending his inferences, interpretations, and judgments. The participants' decisions about when to disclose their unusually personal motivations show that this question needs to be approached in two ways: What is good for the research? And what is healthy for the scholar who is generating that research? This is a complex issue that I hope dissertation Chairs and faculty advisors will approach with both sensitivity and rigor.

Review of Ethical Dilemmas in Unusually Personal Research

- Does having "been there" confer any epistemological advantages to a scholar? If so, how should these be used and reported?
- Does having "been there" confer any threats to the validity of scholarship that purports to be objective, or otherwise mainstream? If so, how should the scholar respond to these threats?
- Responses to threats and advantages will vary depending on the scholar's paradigmatic orientation. Positivists will approach things differently from constructivists.
- If you come into your research with an agenda, how willing are you to change your mind?
- Should you disclose your unusually personal connections to your research? Doing so makes you vulnerable to personal attacks and extra scrutiny. Not doing so makes you more vulnerable to your own bias and limits others' ability to offer emotional, epistemological, or methodological support.

Existential Questions for Readers

1. For researchers: If you have unusually personal connections to your research, have you disclosed these connections to your dissertation committee or other important stakeholders (colleagues, tenure

and promotion committee, etc.)? Why or why not? What are your biggest fears? How might you take steps to avoid these fearful outcomes from coming to fruition? If you cannot avoid them, how could you mitigate them? If you cannot mitigate them, how could you respond to them?

2. For researchers: How could disclosing your unusually personal connections to your research improve your project? Who would be a good person to talk through issues with?
3. For researchers: Have you ever changed your mind about something related to your unusually personal research? If no, is this a problem?
4. For colleagues/advisors: What would you do differently with/for a student or colleague who has an unusually personal motivation for her research project? What validity/trustworthiness concerns would you have?
5. For everyone: Does insider status confer any epistemological advantages for researchers? Do you agree with Montaigne?
6. What do you think about the use of "I" in academic writing? Does avoiding the "I" change anything substantively, or is it just a cosmetic fix?

References

Crenshaw, K. (1989). Demarginalizing the intersection of race and sex: A black feminist critique of antidiscrimination doctrine, feminist theory, and antiracist politics. *University of Chicago Legal Forum, 1*, 139–167.

de Montaigne, M. (1580/2003). *The complete essays* (M. A. Screech, Trans.), Essay 3.13. London: Penguin.

Du Bois, W. E. B. (1887, August). Strivings of the Negro people. *The Atlantic*, p. 197.

Du Bois, W. E. B. (1903/1994). *The souls of black folk*. New York: Dover.

Frankl, V. E. (1946/2014). *Man's search for meaning*. Boston: Beacon Press.

Gonzáles, N., Moll, L. C., & Amanti, C. (2005). *Funds of knowledge: Theorizing practices in households, communities, and classrooms*. New York: Routledge.

Reed-Danahay, D. E. (Ed.). (1997). *Auto/ethnography: Rewriting the self and the social*. New York: Berg.

CHAPTER 9

Franklian Psychology as a Theory of Motivation

All of this suffering and all of this pain—I can give it purpose that way. Just because I'm hurting—I can do something good with it…It's a powerful, painful thought. If I don't share it, it will go to waste because it's just in my head. [If] I write it down, I share it…it becomes alive and it's real and it has a purpose.
—Gillian, Ph.D. Student/Bereavement Researcher, 2007

One thing is crystal clear about the Case Study participants we met in this book. They are *passionate* about their scholarship. This passion came across in their interviews through what they told me, but also through their body language and other paralinguistic cues. There was a contagious emotional intensity to these encounters that made me excited to start writing about them as soon as I got back to my hotel. However, this experience is not unique to these four participants. I have felt the same degree of enthusiasm from speaking with traditionally motivated researchers, especially when I was in graduate school, working among young peers who had not yet found reasons to become jaded about academia. I occasionally find now it among more seasoned colleagues, and it is really fun to talk with these people. This book is dedicated to Sherrie Reynolds, who was one of these. She and I often joked about our perhaps overly enthusiastic propensity to talk about our projects, and in so doing, to "inform others against their will" (Glass and Blumberg 2007). Some of you can relate, I'm sure. There is something I would like to give to other mainstream readers of this book, a way to capture—or

A. Esping, *Epistemology, Ethics, and Meaning in Unusually Personal Scholarship*, https://doi.org/10.1007/978-3-319-73718-8_9

recapture—some of the Case Study participants' enthusiasm for your own work. I aim to offer some data-driven and Frankl-inspired guidance in this chapter.

Passion

The word "passionate" is not a descriptor I chose to characterize the Case Study scholars' work. They chose this word themselves. Across three interviews, Gillian used the word "passion" or "passionate" more than two dozen times to describe her stance toward bereavement research. Jesse and Ron described themselves as being "passionate" researchers nearly one dozen times each. Peggy, who in general was more restrained in expressing emotions during her interviews, used the expression "deep engagement" in much the same way the others used the word passion. She used "engagement" or "deep engagement" five times to explain how she felt about her bioethics work. Here are some representative quotes:

- Gillian, in graduate school, describing how she wanted professors to respond to her: "Encourage…encourage… encouraging me to be **passionate** about it. That it's *okay* to be **passionate**, to own your work. To own your story. To own who you are and why you're there…You know, you don't need to hide it. This is who you are and this is why you're here".
- Jesse describing his response to a professor's feedback after a class presentation: "I was pretty **passionate**. And the feedback that I got from the professor afterwards…the professor said, 'Well you'll learn as you mature in this [field] to provide a more balanced presentation and to not be so overtly [passionate]'…And at the time I thought, 'What the hell's wrong with **passion**? What? Huh?'"
- Ron telling me about his motivation for building a time machine: "You have to remember this was more than a **passion**. It was an obsession."
- Peggy describing why she started writing fiction with bioethics themes: "It's a matter of **deeper engagement**. The death and dying stuff had become somehow really interesting."

The Case Study participants used this language to describe their emotional orientations toward their own scholarship, but they also used it spontaneously in their responses to my interview questions about advice they would have for junior colleagues or mentees. Here are some examples:

- When I asked Gillian if she would advise graduate students to study something related to their personal pain or advise against it, she said, “If you have the **passion** and the drive to do it, and to keep it up, then yeah, by all means.”
- When I asked Jesse what he would say to a young transgender scholar who wanted to study transgender-related issues, he answered, “I think I would respond differently to different people. I would *not* tell them, ‘Don’t be **passionate**. Be objective.’ I wouldn’t tell them that.”
- Ron told me that one piece of advice he gives to young STEM students considering career options is this: “It should be something you are particularly interested in. That’s important. That you have developed the **passion**. That it’s a dream of yours.”
- Peggy’s advice to graduate students who are choosing dissertation topics is this: “It should be something you are particularly interested in. That’s important. I think that you do more and do it better if there is **deeper engagement**. So do what interests you, right? That would be my advice. Do what really interests you.”

The word “passion” has some interesting historical roots, and I think these can illuminate some reasons why the Case Study participants found this word so helpful for explaining their level of commitment to their scholarship. The etymology of “passion” comes from classical Latin, and its original meanings were related to physical pain, suffering, and submission. (Think of the graphic 2004 film, *The Passion of the Christ*.) The earliest uses of the word, beginning in the late 1100s AD, refer to this first definition. By the middle 1200s, “passion” was being used to denote suffering through martyrdom, or general suffering of any kind. About a quarter century later, people were using the word more broadly to describe intense emotional states. Both Chaucer and Shakespeare used “passion” in this sense. It was not until the middle 1600s that the definition moved toward its modern meaning, “an intense desire or enthusiasm *for* something; the zealous pursuit of an aim.” By the 1700s, “passion” had come to mean “an aim or object pursued with zeal; a thing arousing intense enthusiasm” (Oxford English Dictionary, n.d.).

I believe the Case Study participants were using the word "passion" in its modern sense, to mean that they felt intense enthusiasm and zeal for their scholarship. However, I also believe the etymology of the word can help to explain why they felt this way. Clearly, there is something intrinsic to human nature that links pain with purpose. The concept of the "wounded healer" is one way to conceptualize this. The idea is an ancient one, with roots in both Greek mythology and shamanism. In modern times, it is seen as a foundation for 12-step programs and other peer support groups (see Esping 2013). In these contexts, individuals who have demonstrated success in overcoming significant personal adversity take responsibility for helping others who are just getting started in the healing process (e.g., Alcoholics Anonymous 1957). A comprehensive review by Jackson (2001, pp. 1–2) defined a wounded healer this way:

> a person whose personal experience of illness and/or trauma has left lingering effects…in the form of lessons learned that later serve constructive purposes, in the form of attitudes and sensitivities that recurrently serve them in ministering to those whom they treat, or in the form of symptoms or characteristics that stay with them and usefully influence their therapeutic endeavors. That is to say, these healers' own experiences as sufferers may have an enhancing or useful effect on their healing capacities.

The wounded healer phenomenon might explain why the Case Study participants were so passionate about their scholarship. Their experiences of irretrievable loss and unavoidable suffering—two components of Frankl's tragic triad—had gifted them with "attitudes and sensitivities" that could be used constructively to help others. They said as much when they proclaimed the value of their insider understanding, or when they stated their desire to help others from their identity groups—the bereaved, the atypically gendered, families impacted by devastating illness. They had gone through hell and come out the other side, and they wanted to walk with those who were still on the journey. Without using the phrase, I think they were proclaiming themselves wounded healers. Had they chosen a more hands-on approach they might have taken clinical positions instead of academic ones: For example, Peggy's younger sister became a hospice nurse. Perhaps the academic route the Case Study participants chose let them help others while keeping a bit more emotional distance.

Whatever its manifestation—clinical or academic—the wounded healer orientation is profoundly motivating for the helper, and perhaps that is why it has been around for millennia. It is essentially a logotherapeutic idea. When wounded healers acknowledge that their difficult life experiences have conferred something of value to other people, they are exercising an attitudinal value. When they use these insights to sponsor new recovering alcoholics, visit recently diagnosed cancer patients, or research and write about bereavement, the atypically gendered, or end-of-life decision making, they are exercising creative values. The resilience they discover in themselves through this work is an experiential value. This is healing through meaning. This is logotherapy.

Meaning, Motivation, and the Rest of Us

Let's go back to some questions I posed at the end of Chapter 6. Reader, what makes your scholarship meaningful for you? In what ways is it helping you to realize creative, experiential, or attitudinal values? If you are already a faculty member, would you have answered these questions differently when you were in graduate school? Is your work more or less meaningful than it was back then?

My guess is that when you were in graduate school you thought a lot about what to study for your dissertation. This is such an important decision! What role, if any, did your personal uniqueness play in your choice? You probably did not know about Frankl's formulation of disposition, situation, and position when you were working on your Ph.D., but at that time did you consider the possibility that you had something different and special to offer your field because of who you are and where you came from? Did you feel any sense of responsibility to use your uniqueness to create something of value? Did you consider what you would receive in the form of meaningful experiences and emotions through this work? Did you consciously choose an attitude toward your particular set of life and personal circumstances in graduate school? What did you hope you would feel grateful for when it was all over?

If you considered some of these questions, good for you! Most likely, however, this was not your line of reasoning. This is not how we are taught think when choosing dissertation topics. In fact, it would probably be considered by some to be arrogant or even absurd to think this way. What does a new graduate student really know about what the field needs, yet alone what she has to offer the field? Instead, you were probably invited to enter into a symbiotic relationship with a senior researcher, akin to a remora fish and a shark (do a Google image search. It's pretty cool), or you discovered a hole in the existing literature and with guidance you found a way to fill it. This is what deemed your efforts valuable. Along the way, you might have been encouraged to think about what topics are "hot" in your field and to carefully consider the ways in which your topic and methodological approach would position you for the competitive academic job market. Once you made a decision, you kept at it until you demonstrated competence in the knowledge, skills, and dispositions deemed essential in your field. The finished product is your Ph.D. It's a very goal-oriented and efficient process.

There is nothing really wrong with this. It is in many ways a wonderful system. Personally, I loved graduate school, and I think I was immersed in a fairly traditional social science program. However, I would like to propose that those questions about how you are unique and how you can exercise creative, experiential, and attitudinal values through your scholarship are not absurd or arrogant. Indeed, from a Franklian perspective, they are necessary components of an existentially healthy approach to building a long, meaningful, and generative life in the academy. Remember the adaptation presented previously of a key tenet of logotherapy:

> *A researcher's mental health depends—in part—on an awareness of meaning in her scholarship.*

Rather than being arrogant to consider the opportunities inherent in ones' own uniqueness, it is actually a very humble stance toward the privilege of being able to earn a Ph.D. There are many who would love the experience, but few are in the position to attempt it. There are certainly plenty of people for whom it is not a realistic option, including those who cannot afford it, those who have to prioritize family and work obligations, and those who do not possess the necessary attributes to be admitted into a program. Frankl would suggest that those of us who made it have a responsibility to use the opportunity for something meaningful. Here is how he put it:

> Man should not ask what he may expect from life, but should rather understand that life expects something from him...Man should not ask 'What is the meaning of my life?' but should realize that he himself is being questioned. Life is putting its problems to him, and it is up to him to respond to these questions by being responsible; he can only answer to life by answering for his life. (Frankl 1955/1986, p. xxi)

Consider the difference between these two questions:

- What is a unique and valuable topic I could study in my field?
- How does my uniqueness position me to contribute something of value to my field?

Which question, if either, best represents the kind of thinking you were encouraged to do in graduate school? Which question, if either, represents how you go about choosing your research agenda now? Consider the differences in the way these questions would guide a young scholar's thinking and practice. Which question would be most likely to lead to a life in the academy that is both professionally and personally meaningful? Which one would be the most motivating when things got difficult? What would be the motivational impact of considering both of these questions on an ongoing basis?

Recall from Chapter 6 that Frankl claimed that the will to meaning is the most powerful motivational force in human beings (Frankl 1946/2014). In his own case, he believed that the meaning he discovered in his two goals of (1) reconstructing his stolen manuscript and (2) writing about the concentration camp from the perspective of an imprisoned psychiatrist, kept him from dying in the camps (Frankl 1946/2014, 1995/2000). Certainly, the meanings the Case Study participants found through their scholarship helped them to find purpose in the academy and keep moving forward in their careers despite many personal and professional challenges. The meanings you discover in your own work can do this for you, also, even if your personal and professional challenges are far more mundane (see Esping 2010).

Happiness, Power, and Success

Happiness. Power. Success. These pursuits seem to be core values in the USA generally, and they certainly play an important role in people's decisions to enter, and remain in, graduate school and the professoriate. The "pursuit of happiness" has been deemed one of our inalienable human rights, so we feel entitled to feel happy, at least some of the time. If you are not happy in your job, it is likely that you've thought of leaving. The pursuit of success is perhaps particularly salient for the competitive, perfectionistic individuals who are drawn to academia, a system which views itself as a meritocracy. There are many markers of success in academe, tenure and promotion being two of the most important. As for power, that is part of the reason we get Ph.Ds in the first place. Many of us possess the skills to be autodidacts, as arguably that is a lot of what we do when creating the literature reviews that frame our original scholarship. If we were just curious about ideas, we would just read a lot of deep books and talk to other smart people. (A favorite quote from Matt Damon's character to the arrogant Harvard student in the 1997 film, *Good Will Hunting*: "You just spent 150 grand on an education you could have gotten for $1.50 in late fees at the public library.") Those three letters behind our names represent cultural capital that translates into power to influence our students, our fields, and if we decide it is important, the general public.[1]

Frankl's clinical experience, however, lead him to conclude that seeking happiness for the sake of happiness, or success and power for their own sakes will ultimately be unfulfilling. There will always be another goal to chase that you think will make you happier or more successful. Once you achieve that goal, there will be another one. And another one. But *why*? To borrow from a popular documentary title, that is a race to nowhere. Frankl described people in this state this way:

> They exhibit a need for speed. To them, driving a fast car becomes an end in itself. This is a defense mechanism, an attempt to escape the confrontation with an existential vacuum. The less one is aware of a goal the faster he tries to cover the road. The famous Viennese comedian Qualtinger, playing the part of a hooligan, sat on a motorcycle and sang, "It is true, I have no idea where I am going, but anyway, I am getting there faster". (Frankl 1969/2014, pp. 72–73)

What academics should focus on then is a reason, a purpose, or, as Ron put it, a "mission" for their scholarship. There will always be challenging times in academia when we will not feel happy, successful,

[1] I worked a retail job for about a year when I was working on my Ph.D. At the time, I was also teaching two sections of an undergraduate course at the university. The differences in the ways people treated me in these two contexts really brought home the value of a Ph.D.—or even the potential for one—in having influence and being treated with respect. I was the same person with the apron and the name badge as I was in my professional attire walking around the university. However, the difference in how undergraduates perceived me, hence, treated me, in these two milieus was staggering. Make no mistake. Those three letters confer power.

or powerful. Sometimes unavoidable and sad things happen in our universities that make us unhappy. Sometimes our success is thwarted by external circumstances (think budget cuts). Sometimes, like after receiving a mean-spirited peer review, we feel anything but powerful. If happiness, success, and power are your goals, then it is hard to keep motivated when these things happen. Your scholarship is likely to feel less rewarding, and your productivity may take a temporary dive because you failed at achieving your goal of feeling happy or being successful. In contrast, a meaning orientation will pull us forward productively through good times and bad. Let's look at what Frankl said about this. On happiness:

> It is a characteristic of the American culture that, again and again, one is commanded and ordered to "be happy." But happiness cannot be pursued; it must ensue. One must have a reason to "be happy." Once the reason is found however, one becomes happy automatically….A human being is not one in pursuit of happiness but rather in search of a reason to become happy, last but not least, through actualizing the potential meaning inherent and dormant in a given situation. (Frankl 1946/2014, p. 130)

Of success, he said:

> Don't aim at success—the more you aim at it and make it a target, the more you are going to miss it. For success, like happiness, cannot be pursued; it must ensue, and it only does so as the unintended side-effect of one's personal dedication to a cause greater than oneself or as the by-product of one's surrender to a person other than oneself. Happiness must happen, and the same holds for success: you have to let it happen by not caring about it…Listen to what your conscience commands you to do and go on to carry it out to the best of your knowledge. Then you will live to see that in the long run…success will follow you precisely because you had forgotten to think of it. (Frankl 1946/1984, p. 17)

In essence, he is saying here that happiness, success, and power will feel existentially empty so long as they are made the primary focus of one's existence. A truly happy, successful, and powerful human being will feel fulfilled because she committed to a goal that is larger than the happiness, success, or power itself. If the goal that you think will make you happy, successful, or powerful is graduating with a Ph.D., landing a tenure-track job, getting tenure, or getting published in a particular journal, you might want to rethink how this achievement will actually function for you existentially. Your life isn't over once you reach that goal. If that was your reason for working hard, you will eventually have to find another goal to fill up the space that took up in your head. And then you are on a hamster wheel, or just creating widget after widget in the scholarship factory until you retire. That's no way to live. What if, instead, you chose a meaningful commitment to something larger than yourself, and in working hard to leave that legacy you achieved success, happiness, or power? How would this attitude make your present life in the academy more meaningful?

I realize that some of this advice might seem unrealistic. For a host of completely understandable reasons, you are not at liberty to make any drastic changes in your existential quest to live a meaningful academic life. Some of you may be stuck on projects that you are not excited about, but you must follow through. Tenure requirements can be daunting, and there are times when you just have to pump out those widgets. Here is what I have to say to you: You are in precisely the situation that Frankl was most passionate about helping with. Logotherapy—that is, finding healing through meaning—is perhaps most therapeutic when external freedoms are limited. Think of Frankl's situation in the camps. He couldn't make any big changes either. But he could change his ***attitude*** toward his situation. Remember, the ability to choose one's attitude toward an unchangeable circumstance is "the last of human freedoms" (Allport 1984, p. 12). Exercising attitudinal values is always possible. So, Reader, if this is your situation, Frankl would ask you to try to choose a position. What meanings can you discover in the work you are doing? Is it helping to pay for your child's schooling? Are you able to offer a smile or a cup of coffee to the department's underappreciated administrative assistant? Can you utilize contacts developed through your unfulfilling project to launch a new line of research? What opportunities do you have that you might have overlooked?

One last thing. If you are uncomfortable with the comparison between Frankl's horrific imprisonment in the death camps and getting paid to conduct unfulfilling scholarship, take heart. I am not comparing. If the therapeutic potential of logotherapy rested on a comparison between our lives and Frankl's, the framework would be completely ineffectual, because for the vast majority of people there is no comparison to make. Franklian existential psychology maintains that the search for meaning, being a healthy, natural, and necessary part of human existence, is available to everyone, in good circumstances and in bad (Frankl 1946/2014). It's just that in good circumstances, we sometimes forget that we need it.

Implications for Advising

To minimize the direct pursuit of happiness, success, and power, graduate students should be encouraged to stay in touch with the meaning orientation that brought them to school in the first place. Faculty should advise students early on that they should expect their specific academic and life goals to change, and support them as they transition to new goals by keeping them focused on what they can do with their degrees, rather than what their degrees can do for them. (I am reminded of the popular quote often attributed to Spiderman's Uncle Ben: "With great power comes great responsibility.") The ongoing and fluid discovery of meaning should be talked about unabashedly, which means that we in academia must learn to balance a desire for scientific rigor with acknowledgment that it is healthy and existentially important to have a passionate commitment to a research topic. It is to this we now turn.

Being Passionate and Being Objective

This chapter began by exploring the significance of the word "passionate" to describe the Case Study participants' powerful motivation for their scholarship. Before concluding I would like to point out one more way in which the social scientist, Jesse, used this word. In his interviews, he set up "passion" and "objectivity" as binary opposites. Here are two examples. The first is an excerpt from his answer when I asked him what advice he might give a young transgender scholar. He told me, "I would *not* tell them, 'Don't be passionate. Be objective.'" The second example comes from his internal response to the professor who told him to tone down his passion for class presentations:

> Why *should* I temper my passion? And I *have*...some pretty strong opinions. And I'm going to try to find empirical evidence to support my opinions. And that's no different than any other scientist. That's no different than somebody studying bacteria. You know, they *have* a theory that they feel pretty strongly about or they wouldn't go to the time and expense

and trouble to test it. And of *course* they're going to run tests…that they believe are going to support their theories. And when it doesn't get supported you report that…Why should I tone down my rhetoric just to *appear* more objective? I mean, is anyone really objective? I don't think so. The guy studying bacteria is not objective. He's trying to find evidence for his theories.

Social scientists have sometimes been accused of having physics envy (Clarke and Primo 2012), which essentially means we are insecure about our epistemologies, or perhaps just insecure about what scholars in the hard sciences will think about our epistemologies, so we overuse jargon and otherwise try to make our work look as "sciency" as possible. The common admonition in academic work to avoid the use of the first person "I" in favor of third person "the researcher" is probably a manifestation of this. Sometimes this makes no sense at all, other than to paint an objective veneer on an article that would be substantively the same either way. Perhaps disavowing passion for our work is also part of physics envy.

Jesse sees himself as a postpositivist, which for him means objectivity is a worthy, but probably unattainable goal. He does not believe passion is incongruous with the attempt at objectivity, but he does seem to think other social scientists *do* believe this. And he is right. Since the Enlightenment, researchers have been cautioned to avoid topics in which they have a large personal investment in the outcome (see Dittmann 2005; Mooney 1957). The main reason is that positivist-leaning, mainstream social science views personal investment as a threat to the validity of any publication that purports to be empirical (see Denzin and Lincoln 2003; Ellis 2004; Mooney 1957). Personally, I have received this message too: If you care too much, the rigor of your scholarship is suspect. It is much more professional to cultivate or feign emotional detachment. Ironically, theoretical physicist Ron did not see passion for ones work as being at all incompatible with rigor or objectivity. Indeed, he expressed genuine surprise when I mentioned to him that some scholars I know believe they need to hide their passion in order to be taken seriously. He thought his passion had no bearing on how others view his physics work, as the equations speak for themselves. Moreover, the field as a whole respects—even expects—passion from its members. Here is what he said about this:

Oh no! See it's the opposite in physics! As a matter of fact it's the *intensity* of it. In fact, it's what has led to divorces, and has led to nervous

> breakdowns. But it's the extent to which [theoretical physicists] put their passion out there on the table…This is a priesthood…This is actually a *calling*, this is not an occupation. And we're all in this calling together, so we appreciate what goes into that calling.

So I wonder, reader, if objectivity is your goal, is this goal incompatible with feeling passion for your work?

Conclusions

Scholarship, unusually personal and otherwise, can be a very passionate endeavor. Gillian, Jesse, Ron, and Peggy certainly experienced their work in this way. Part of the reason may be that one of their altitudinal values was conceptualizing themselves as wounded healers who had something of unique value to contribute to the academy. Passion, after all, originally referred to pain. Through their contributions, they gradually achieved success and power, and at times, happiness. But their meaning orientation kept them at it even when this was not the case. If meaning is your goal, then temporarily feeling unhappy, unsuccessful, or weak will not stop you from moving forward. That perspective can benefit the rest of us who work in the academy. Let's challenge the traditional academic hegemony and choose to ask big existential questions about our scholarship. How are you unique? What is your responsibility? What can you create, experience, and choose? We can be passionate researchers and still pay careful attention to issues of validity, and if it is important in your discipline, objectivity. It's time we stopped thinking of passion and objectivity as binary opposites and embraced the idea that it need not be naïve or dangerous to be excited about our scholarship.

Review of Frankl's Existential Psychology as a Theory of Motivation

- The word "passion" is related to suffering. When you follow the changing meanings of "passion" over time, it seems clear that there is something intrinsic to human nature that links pain with purpose.
- Wounded healers are people who use their personal experiences with adversity to help others. Often the others they help are part

of their own identity group. The role of the sponsor in 12-Step programs is an example of this. The concept of the wounded healer is ancient. Present-day scholars can be wounded healers too.

- Becoming a wounded healer can feel therapeutic because it provides a way to exercise creative, experiential, and attitudinal values.
- Do not make happiness, success, or power your goals. If you do, these achievements will eventually feel empty. Instead, choose to find meaning in your work, and let happiness, success, and power come as by-products of your existential goal. Think of it this way: You don't need to be happy or successful or powerful. What you need is a reason to be happy, successful, or powerful.
- The search for meaning is especially helpful when you are not at liberty to make big external changes. Remember, you can always change your attitude toward your unchangeable circumstances. This is the last of human freedoms.
- Do not worry about comparing your experience to Frankl's experience in the camps. That is a ridiculous comparison, and we all know it. It is not necessary. Logotherapy is useful for everyone.
- You can be passionate about your research and still value objectivity. These are not binary opposites.

Existential Questions for Readers

1. How do you weigh the value of personal meaning and professional advancement when choosing a scholarly project? Are these opposites, or do they complement each other?
2. Could you become more productive if you felt like your scholarship was more meaningful? What might this look like? How does focusing on meaning differ from focusing on productivity? How would the outcomes differ?
3. Would you feel weird telling a colleague that you were "passionate" about your scholarship? Why? What does your answer reveal about the academic culture you inhabit?
4. Is there any way in which your scholarship could be conceptualized as being founded on the concept of the "wounded healer"? How so?
5. Do you believe that you are directly pursuing happiness, success, or power through your scholarship? Or are you letting these things ensue? Does the difference feel like it would matter in your case?

References

Alcoholics Anonymous. (1957). *Alcoholics anonymous*. New York: Alcoholics Anonymous Publishing.

Allport, G. (1984). Preface. In V. Frankl (Au.), *Man's search for meaning* (pp. 9–13). New York: Pocket Books.

Clarke, K. A., & Primo, D. M. (2012, March 30). Overcoming "physics envy". *The New York Times Sunday Review*. Available at: http://www.nytimes.com/2012/04/01/opinion/sunday/the-social-sciences-physics-envy.html.

Denzin, N. K., & Lincoln, Y. S. (Eds.). (2003). *The landscape of qualitative research: Theories and issues* (2nd ed.). Thousand Oaks, CA: Sage.

Dittmann, M. (2005). Starting the dissertation: Experts offer tips on picking a topic, conducting a lit review and narrowing your focus. *GradPsych, 3*(1), 20–23.

Ellis, C. (2004). *The ethnographic I: A methodological novel about autoethnography*. Walnut Creek, CA: AltaMira.

Esping, A. (2010). Motivation in doctoral programs: A logotherapeutic perspective. *The International Forum for Logotherapy, 33*(2), 72–78.

Esping, A. (2013). From "at-risk" youth to wounded Healer: A longitudinal study of two preservice teachers. *International Journal for Qualitative Studies in Education, 26*(5), 1–20.

Frankl, V. E. (1946/1984/2014). *Man's search for meaning*. Boston: Beacon Press.

Frankl, V. E. (1955/1986). *The doctor and the soul*. New York: Vintage Books.

Frankl, V. E. (1969/2014). *The will to meaning: Foundations and applications of logotherapy*. New York: Meridian.

Frankl, V. E. (1995/2000). *Recollections: An autobiography* (J. Fabry & J. Fabry, Trans.). Cambridge: Basic Books.

Glass, I., & Blumberg, A. (Producers). (2007, February 16). *Quiz Show* [Radio broadcast]. In *This American Life*. Chicago, IL: National Public Radio.

Jackson, S. W. (2001). The wounded healer. *Bulletin of the History of Medicine, 75*, 1–36.

Mooney, R. L. (1957). The researcher himself. In *Research for curriculum improvement, Association for Supervision and Curriculum Development, 1957 yearbook* (pp. 153–186). Washington D.C.: Association for Supervision and Curriculum Development.

Passion. (n.d.). *Oxford English Dictionary online*. Retrieved October 2017 from http://www.oed.com.

CHAPTER 10

The Search for Meaning in the Academy

In the academy we do not create résumés. We build vitas.
In Latin the word vita *means "life".*

One of the important images derived from Frankl's work—that of his vision of himself at the podium in a "well-lit, warm and pleasant lecture room" after liberation—has served as a key metaphor throughout this book. I believe Gillian, Jesse, Ron, and Peggy are standing at their own podiums in the well-lit rooms of the academy. Scholarship has helped them understand their painful—in some cases, tragic—life experiences, and their painful life experiences have contributed meaningfully to their scholarship. Like Frankl, they are content-area academic experts who also have a passionate and visceral understanding of the phenomena they study. Their insider status makes them unique, and they have embraced the opportunities presented by their singular perspectives. This can be a powerful and controversial epistemological stance.

While I believe it is going too far to say that their academic goals helped them to survive, as Frankl's did, I think it is fair to say that the meaning they discovered in their academic goals improved their lives. This might be enough to deem their scholarship important and valuable. But I think it would also be a true statement to say that their scholarship has also improved the lives of others. They could have curled up on the couch and quit. Instead, they spoke at conferences, taught courses, and authored

A. Esping, *Epistemology, Ethics, and Meaning in Unusually Personal Scholarship*, https://doi.org/10.1007/978-3-319-73718-8_10

journal articles and books. They created beautiful and meaningful lives, and the iterative relationship between their personal experiences and their scholarship was an important part of this journey. Despite the diverse ways in which these individuals arrived at the synergy of painful lived experience and serious academic work, I believe they share a common future. Their ongoing publications, presentations, and teaching will, as Viktor Frankl suggested, "bear witness to the uniquely human potential at its best, which is to transform a personal tragedy into a triumph, to turn one's predicament into human achievement" (Frankl 1946/2014, p. 105).

The Future of the Well-Lit Room

The title of this book has the phrase "unusually personal" in it, but I'm not sure this kind of work is really all that unusual. Wherever I have a chance to talk about this project, I am approached by scholars who are eager to share a story about themselves or a colleague who could have been included here. Some of the people who share these stories with me have not previously discussed them, out of concerns that they will be seen as "too biased" or because doing so would make them feel emotionally vulnerable in professional settings. Others have always been outspoken about their personal connections to their scholarship, and they are glad to find a community of like-minded souls. You may have a story of your own. If so, I would love to hear it! I have set up a Facebook page, "The Well-lit Room," for this purpose.

There are also quite a few prominent researchers who have been writing and speaking about the synergy and tension between their lived experience and their academic work. Here are three examples, representing the Ivy League: One of the most dynamic researchers in my own field is Scott Barry Kaufman, a leading cognitive psychologist and expert in human intelligence and creativity. Diagnosed at an early age with a learning disability, he repeated third grade and spent years in special education. He received his Ph.D. from Yale. In the prologue to his 2013 book, *Ungifted: The Truth about Talent, Practice, Creativity, and the Many Paths to Greatness*, he separates "Subjective Scott" from "Objective Scott" to demonstrate the different ways his life experience and research experience clarify and obfuscate controversial topics related to IQ. Another example is Hugh Herr, who directs the Biomechatronics group at the Massachusetts Institute of Technology (MIT) Media Lab.

Herr is a double amputee who studies the ways electromechanics and human physiology can work together to create bionic limbs. He has authored more than 150 peer-reviewed articles and patents, and he is also a user of the technology he helps to develop (Willyard 2007). Finally, there is Jill Bolte Taylor, who suffered a left-hemisphere stroke a year after completing postdoctoral fellowships in neuroscience and psychiatry at Harvard. Her 2006 book, *Stroke of Insight: A Brain Scientist's Personal Journey*, describes what a professional neuroanatomist can learn from temporarily losing the ability to walk, talk, read, write, and remember.

Another thing that happens when I talk about this project is people ask me what my own story is. Considering that my research focuses on people who have painful personal connections to their research, they assume I must also. This sounds so splendidly "meta." Truthfully, the origins of this work do not come from my own life, except that as a first-generation college student I have always been preternaturally fascinated by the academic world I inhabit. Its norms and values are something I have always observed closely, as if from the outside. I have also always been super excited to be here. Post-tenure I am still kind of surprised that I get to do this for a living. So, reader, I don't have a beautiful personal story to share with you. But this brings back an important point from Chapter 9: You don't *have* to have a painful story to build a deeply meaningful career in academia. The existential perspective that worked so well for Gillian, Jesse, Ron, and Peggy works for me too. And a change to a more existential perspective can help you, too, if at present you are not currently feeling particularly fulfilled or successful in academia. Focus on your uniqueness. Find your responsibility. Exercise creative, experiential, and attitudinal values. Happiness and success will come simply because you've stopped looking for them.

It strikes me as poetic that academia we don't create résumés, but build vitas. *Curriculum Vitae* literally means "the course of one's life" in Latin (Oxford English Dictionary, n.d.). When we shorten it and say "my vita," we are saying "my life." So when you put something on your vita, you are adding it to an account of your life. Few professions offer the opportunity to integrate the personal and the professional so fully.

A final metaphor, this one from Viktor Frankl (1969/2014, p. 94): "Your life is a monument." Choose now what you want to leave behind. Begin with the end in mind.

Existential Questions for Readers

1. Pull up a copy of your CV. How does translating *curriculum vitae* to “the course of one’s life” change the way you look at that document?
2. Pretend that today is the day you retire from academia. How will your colleagues remember you after you have gone? What will your field, your department, or your students miss because you are not there? Is there anything you want to change about this now?

References

Curriculum vitae. (n.d.). *Oxford English Dictionary online.* Retrieved October 2017 from http://www.oed.com.

Frankl, V. E. (1946/1984/2014). *Man’s search for meaning.* Boston: Beacon Press.

Frankl, V. E. (1969/2014). *The will to meaning: Foundations and applications of logotherapy.* New York: Meridian.

Kaufman, S. B. (2013). *Ungifted: The truth about talent, practice, creativity, and the many paths to greatness.* Cambridge: Basic Books.

Taylor, J. B. (2006). *My stroke of insight: A brain scientist’s personal journey.* New York: Plume.

Willyard, C. (2007). Profile: Hugh Herr. *Nature Medicine, 13,* 1395.

Index

A. Esping, *Epistemology, Ethics, and Meaning in Unusually Personal Scholarship*, https://doi.org/10.1007/978-3-319-73718-8

The manufacturer's authorised representative in the EU is Springer Nature Customer Service Centre GmbH, Europaplatz 3, 69115 Heidelberg, Germany. If you have any concerns regarding our products, please contact ProductSafety@springernature.com

Printed and bound by CPI Group (UK) Ltd, Croydon, CR0 4YY
28/11/2025
02007705-0001